Queer Pleasure Without Apology

SUNY series in Queer Politics and Cultures
―――――――
Cynthia Burack and Jyl J. Josephson, editors

Queer Pleasure Without Apology

GREG GOLDBERG

Cover lithograph by Paul Cézanne, *The Large Bathers* (*Les Baigneurs*), 1898. The Metropolitan Museum of Art, New York, bequest of Scofield Thayer, Estate of Scofield Thayer, 1984, www.metmuseum.org.

Published by State University of New York Press, Albany

© 2025 State University of New York

All rights reserved

Printed in the United States of America

No part of this book may be used or reproduced in any manner whatsoever without written permission. No part of this book may be stored in a retrieval system or transmitted in any form or by any means including electronic, electrostatic, magnetic tape, mechanical, photocopying, recording, or otherwise without the prior permission in writing of the publisher.

Links to third-party websites are provided as a convenience and for informational purposes only. They do not constitute an endorsement or an approval of any of the products, services, or opinions of the organization, companies, or individuals. SUNY Press bears no responsibility for the accuracy, legality, or content of a URL, the external website, or for that of subsequent websites.

EU GPSR Authorised Representative:
Logos Europe, 9 rue Nicolas Poussin, 17000, La Rochelle, France
contact@logoseurope.eu

For information, contact State University of New York Press, Albany, NY
www.sunypress.edu

Library of Congress Cataloging-in-Publication Data

Name: Goldberg, Greg, author.
Title: Queer pleasure without apology / Greg Goldberg.
Description: Albany : State University of New York Press, [2025] | Series: SUNY series in queer politics and cultures | Includes bibliographical references and index.
Identifiers: LCCN 2024049452 | ISBN 9798855802764 (hardcover : alk. paper) | ISBN 9798855802788 (ebook) | ISBN 9798855802771 (pbk. : alk. paper)
Subjects: LCSH: Gay men—Sexual behavior—United States. | Cruising (Sexual behavior)—United States. | Sexual excitement—United States.
Classification: LCC HQ76.115 .G65 2025 | DDC 306.77086/642—dc23/eng/20250131
LC record available at https://lccn.loc.gov/2024049452

For those whose names I didn't catch

Contents

Acknowledgments ix

Prologue: Filthy Little Pig xi

Chapter 1   The Defense Rests   1

Chapter 2   Impersonal Intimacy   19

Chapter 3   Labels Are for People   43

Chapter 4   Masc for Masc   57

Chapter 5   Abject Objects   77

Chapter 6   Meet Markets   87

Chapter 7   Plaything   101

Notes   117

Bibliography   135

Index   145

Acknowledgments

Thank you to Leo Altafini, Robyn Autry, Ted Baab, Daniel Barrow, Chiara Bercu, Patricia Clough, Rebecca Colesworthy, Jonathan Cutler, Denise Ficker, Isabel Goldberg, Mark Goldberg, Katie Halper, Erik Hane, Bryan Jagoe, Kate Levin, Cayden Lovejoy, Tom Roach, James Rubin, Rachel Schiff, Chris Stedman, Rita Strauss, Michelle Tea, Craig Willse, Andrea Wu, "Jeremy," all my "Bad Sex" students over the years, and my peer reviewers.

Portions of Chapters 1, 2, and 6 were developed in earlier articles: "Lust Room" (*GLQ* 31, no. 1, 2025) and "Meet Markets" (*Convergence* 26, no. 2, 2020). I am grateful to both journals—their editors, boards, staff, and reviewers—for publishing them.

Prologue
Filthy Little Pig

"Hate that I've never even visited New York and am forced to know about some obscure cruising spot being turned into a parking lot. Personally I think we as gay people should stop having sex outside like animals but that's just me."[1]

I should not have been so irritated by this tweet from a self-identified "left-wing eye-roller."[2] I should not have taken it seriously. I should not have let it get under my skin. I should not have thought about it for as long as I did. I should not have felt so betrayed by a stranger. I should not have spent so long considering how to respond. I should not have been baited so easily into an argument.

I wanted to defend cruising and public sex as central parts of US gay culture.[3] I wanted to call this writer homophobic. I wanted to call him a traitor. I wanted to accuse him of having bad politics. I wanted to dismiss him—a young, gay man living in the Florida Panhandle—as envious. I wanted to point out the incompatibility of this stance with other things he'd written. I wanted to draw attention to the convenience of making his own sexual desires the standard according to which he judges other people. I wanted to mock his moralizing language ("like animals"), and his cliché passive-aggressiveness ("but that's just me"). In truth, I wanted to make him feel ashamed of what he wrote, as ashamed as I'd been made to feel for desiring public sex—not just by him, but by an entire culture—for much of my life. Hypocritically, I wanted to shame him for shaming. I wanted to tell him (and everyone like him) to fuck off. You might say he touched a nerve.

I didn't do any of this. Something else clicked for me, and instead I replied, "I'm a filthy little pig, aren't I? Tell me again." Instead of arguing with him, I agreed with him. At the risk of overexplaining a joke: I implicated him as an actor in the eroticism of cruising and public sex, that is, the disgusted onlooker who makes possible the pleasure of transgression. We're all in this together. It's not how he meant his statement to be taken, but to do something new with people, you sometimes have to take things differently, as Eve Sedgwick demonstrated decades ago. Yes, I am an animal, and more specifically a pig.[4] We may be fighting, but are you sure we're not also flirting? His response was encouraging: "LOL."

The tragedy of coming out, for me, was not that it never ends, or that it unnecessarily or insidiously congeals fluid desire into static identity—true as these may be—but that it doesn't get to the heart of the matter. High school notwithstanding, my desire to have sex with men has not been difficult for me to claim publicly, given my social location. It is the more specific contours of my desire that are a problem, not just for conservatives, but for many on the supposedly tolerant left, even the progressive, sex-positive, queer and feminist left.[5] If I am a slut, I should be an "ethical slut"[6]; as a masculine-presenting cisgender man, I should not erotically discriminate against feminine men; I should not fetishize other social groups; I should not enjoy seducing my objects of desire, nor should I discard them when I grow bored, unless I'm punching up, and maybe not even then. So many restrictions and provisos.

Not so long ago, legible homosexuality would have been enough to make a guy like me—privileged in many other ways—an outsider in the US.[7] Not so much anymore. Where I'm from, "gay" is mostly an innocuous biographical detail. I know that it's foolish to romanticize the homophobic past.[8] I know that I owe my wider sphere of sexual freedom, in part, to a diverse group of gay, queer, and trans activists who fought for decades against legal persecution, social discrimination, and medical neglect, drawing, in part, from the anti-racist, anti-war, and feminist movements, as Roderick E. Ferguson details.[9] Gay liberation paved the way for a normative gay identity for people like me, should we be willing to accept it.[10] "Queer" then took over the work of describing those misfits who could not or would not assimilate. In 1990, when queer theory was coalescing as a field, the term "queer" still "carried a high voltage charge of insult and stigma," as Michael Warner writes.[11] But in 2012—the time of Warner's writing—"queer" had already become a "cable-TV synonym for gay." On the left in the US, "queer" is now used in a few basic ways: as an umbrella identity for everyone who is not straight; as a more specific identity for people who are trans or non-binary—or who desire them—and who feel excluded from the cis-leaning sexual categories "straight," "gay," and "bi"; as an identity for anyone—including would-be heterosexuals—with non-normative sexual desires or "lifestyles"; and as a way to signal one's political opposition to gay liberalism and express a commitment to social justice and/or liberation.[12] More colloquially, "queer" is also sometimes used to describe non-straight people with an androgynous or gender-bendy personal style. A gay friend of mine in Brooklyn who favors masculine daddies put it this way, in a dejected tone: "Everyone here is so . . . queer." This definitional expansion has come at the expense of the "nitty-gritty of sexuality," as Teresa De Lauretis observes.[13] If we are going to continue having a conversation about sex that disturbs, we might once again need a new term. I'm partial to "pervert," a term used by Gayle Rubin throughout her canonical essay "Thinking Sex," and which, after all these years, still has a sting about it.

But the point I'm trying to make is not about the terms we use, but rather the "nitty-gritty" of sex that they describe, which is disturbing until it isn't. While some US conservatives are clearly still panicked about homosexuality—Ron DeSantis's "Don't Say Gay" crusade comes to mind—the left has come around on homosexuality to the point that a white, masculine-presenting, middle-class, married, former-military, gay man—Pete Buttigieg—could viably run for president in 2020. Most non-queer people on the left are now more than happy to say "gay" and even to joke about tops and bottoms (as in the 2013 *Saturday Night Live* sketch "Who's on Top?"), although they sometimes inadvertently reveal that they find bottoming undesirably degrading.[14] The panic about gender and sexual non-normativity is also turning out to be mostly unwarranted for many on the left in the US. Why not let the people identify how they want to identify? Why not let drag queens read stories to children at public libraries, and consenting adults tie each other up in bed, exchange money for sex, or have multiple partners, if that's what they want? These kinds of non-normativity, it turns out, can be narrated as compatible with the left's ethical commitments. Which brings me back to the contours of desire, my perversions, so-to-speak—the subject of this book.

One should not underestimate the queer left's ability to redescribe troubling sexual desires and pleasures as either benign or virtuous. Yet, the more antisocial one's desires and pleasures are—that is, the more they contradict the left's commitment to the social—the more difficult it is for liberals and progressives alike to accept them. This is not to assume that antisocial sex wants to be accepted. In fact, it may disturb the left precisely because it doesn't want to be accepted. Just because we're depraved doesn't mean we're deprived, though our "allies" may assume the latter. From a left perspective, the granting of sexual identity is a kind of affirmation of one's desires and pleasures: You need gay identity to have gay pride. But from the perspective of antisocial sex—and maybe all sex—the granting of identity is an attempt to cleanse sex of its antisocial elements. In this context, coming out might be less about having one's desires and pleasures accepted and affirmed than about policing sex by suturing it to a legible identity fit for participation in the social.

I'm not trying to be flippant or to romanticize being an outsider, especially given my mostly-insider social position. I know that the consequences of sexual stigma are not evenly distributed across social groups. For example, while I do risk arrest for lewd conduct when I cruise public restrooms, this risk is mitigated by my whiteness—police don't tend to view me with suspicion—my ability to afford adequate legal representation, my status as a US citizen, and my cultural capital. Furthermore, I don't have to endure what Alex Espinoza describes as the "self-surveillance of the brown queer body" while cruising.[15] Even with the reduced risk I face, if forced to choose between stigma and pride, I would choose pride, though it would exact a significant price: the antisocial desires and pleasures that can't be integrated into an identity. More to the point, it's a false choice: stigma and pride are two sides of the same social coin, as queer theory made clear decades ago. Just because I don't want to be arrested doesn't mean I want to be included.

As my appetite for sex has waned with age, my palette has expanded: sex in public bathrooms and parks, unprotected sex with total strangers without so much as a word exchanged, sex with men twenty years my junior or senior, sex with men who are cheating on their spouses, sex with men whose blue-collar masculinity turns me on—the menu is long. Some of this sex roils conservatives, some of it disturbs liberals and progressives, and some of it bothers radicals, even the queer ones. The moralization of sex—declaring that certain desires and behaviors are good or bad—seems designed, in part, to render sex more orderly, whether under the guise of justice or virtue. It attempts to sanitize sex, to cleanse it of disorderly pleasure, to funnel the genuinely disturbing into the merely naughty, a sloppy cleanup operation that draws us precisely to the filth it leaves behind.

Can we have a different conversation about our "bad" desires and pleasures, one that is more curious and playful? This book represents my best effort to respond to this question, to take up this challenge. My hope is that releasing sex from judgment might make (or reestablish) space for a liberationist approach to sex that is not anxious about or fearful of whatever turns us on and gets us off—no justification or apology required. This is less about making stigmatized sex more acceptable than about bypassing the issue of acceptability altogether.

Much academic writing about sex seems geared to tame this unruly object, to get its pleasure under control. As Adam Phillips writes, "In giving an account we make of sexuality, of our desire, something that it is not and can never be. It is as though we are trying to stop it having its effect, prevent it taking its course."[16] What if thinking and writing about sex didn't do this? What if it didn't drain the qualities that make sex such a compelling object to think about in the first place? As Kane Race asks, "What happens when we conceive of our work as thinking *with* pleasure, rather than simply researching pleasure or thinking *about* it?"[17] What if thinking and writing about sex were as stimulating and perplexing as its object? What if it were as uncertain, open-ended, and risky as cruising a stranger at a urinal? What form might such thinking and writing take? What might it allow us to see and feel?

I am inspired by a question asked by Frederick C. Corey and Thomas K. Nakayama: "How is it possible to write in the fulcrum between the language of academia and the language of sex?"[18] This question acquires a particular urgency at the present moment, when queer theory has largely retreated from writing about sex, as Oliver Davis and Tim Dean argue, focusing instead on intersectionality in a way that can paradoxically marginalize sex.[19]

For me, writing between the academic and the sexual is not about attempting to make sex more orderly, though I'm probably drawn to thinking about sex in the first place because of its unruliness.[20] Nor is it about fighting sexual shame or stigma through publicness, though I do sometimes feel politically indignant, and I may be something of an exhibitionist.[21] I expect that some voyeuristic readers may want to read just the salacious bits and skip the rumination, as I too sometimes skim academic writing that includes personal anecdotes—especially sexual ones—for the juicy parts. But my hope is that readers will find both parts not only symbiotic, but also pleasurably stimulating and generative, even if they can't relate to my experience: sexually, socially, or otherwise.

In a discussion of psychologist Evelyn Hooker's 1962 ethnographic article "The Homosexual Community," Heather Love writes that "Hooker's observational style is a method that fits the optical and erotic arrangements of the bar space."[22] I'm not an ethnographer, and I'm generally suspicious of the motives that underlie the production of ethnographic knowledge, not to mention the aspiration to produce objective truths about social groups, which invariably draws my attention more to the scholar trying to vanish in scientific omniscience than to the groups they're attempting to represent.[23] "Pay no attention to that man behind the curtain," the great and powerful Oz commands, knowing full well that the jig is up. Additionally, as Love observes, "Detailed, detached analyses of the folkways of the homosexual can strike an odd note in a moment when queers are doing it for themselves. The dated language, stance of neutrality, and frequent appeals to common sense in postwar research on sexuality suggest a perspective on norms and their violation alien to the explicitly political field of queer studies."[24] That said, I'm tickled by Love's characterization of Hooker's academic voyeurism as consistent with the cruising she observed. Every cruiser begins as an ethnographer of sorts, though unlike ethnographers we don't package our kink in advocacy, and we also know how—in the words of singer-songwriter Iris DeMent—to let the mystery be, at least while we're cruising.

In addition to avoiding a stance of neutrality, one of the analytical virtues of writing about one's own experience is that it may make it easier to identify variation, complexity, and nuance—especially when you're not being attacked, or when you've opted out of defending yourself—where others find only homogeneity. I'm hardly immune to the appeal of writing that goes big, but there is often a cost: a convenient simplification or erasure of details that don't fit the model. At the same time, I'm left unsatisfied by memoiristic accounts that indiscriminately accumulate details where other scholars have painted with an insensitively broad and often critical brush. There is pleasure in apprehending heterogeneity, but my curiosity depends on larger questions and issues that make the specificity of heterogeneous details interesting to me. I'm reminded of Jonathan Flatley's argument (about Andy Warhol's work) that "the field of similarity established by the collected creates a uniquely ideal site for appreciating specificity."[25] As all collectors know, variations tend to stand out in relation to the group to which they've been assigned: shoes, dolls, coins.

The scholars I engage here tend to do this, curating objects of analysis—sexual desires and pleasures, mostly—whose heterogeneity is animated (rather than dulled) by the larger questions in which they're interested. Leo Bersani and Tim Dean are particularly useful because of their interest in impersonal sex, eroticized masculinity, the social world, and psychoanalytic theory, but many other scholars and writers—including Adam Phillips, Andrea Long Chu, Kane Race, Shaka McGlotten, Tom Roach, Eve Sedgwick, and Alex Espinoza—have influenced my thinking; I draw on their empirical observations, social and political provocations, historical accounts, and theoretical vocabularies in considering my own "bad" desires and pleasures. I have curated these desires and pleasures into a kind of collection that aims to make their specificity newly interesting by asking about their larger effects without turning the whole thing into a trial. It is not an exhaustive catalog of pathologized sex. It is not even a complete inventory of my own depravity. Nor is it a demystification or legitimation of that which has been stigmatized—a point that bears emphasizing, as readers may be accustomed to this kind of reversal. Rather, it is an attempt to put together a series of small things—encounters, impressions, observations, feelings, and readings—to think something new about big things—power, identity, knowledge, and our relations with each other.

As a sociologist, I know that it's unwise to make sweeping statements based in and tethered to the specificity of my position and experience. But that specificity, if handled with care, can also provide a foundation from which to interrogate and challenge existing wisdom, and to think differently—queerly, as it were—about the social world. It is inevitable that this process will bear my imprint. For those of us inclined to lose our selves in thought, the trick is to keep this in mind.

Like good sex, my favorite writing moves something around in me, stirs something up, unsettles something in a way that grabs me, makes me nervous, and keeps me coming back for more. And like sex, reading is something you seem to do with another person: an author. It can feel like a conversation as you respond to and argue with an author in the privacy of your mind, but, like sex (according to Phillips), it's ultimately one-sided.[26] It is, perhaps, the most explicitly one-sided relationship that exists, and it teaches us the valuable lesson that feeling seen may have little to do with being seen. How I struggle to communicate the depth of my appreciation when I meet an author or artist whose work I admire, in a futile effort to establish a modicum of reciprocity with them.

To read is to be both in your own head and someone else's hands: mine at the moment. When I read, in order to relax sufficiently and allow a text to work on me, I need to trust the hands I'm in; to not have to know where a path leads, to be able to question a sacred thing, to believe that I can survive my own transformation. To write is to approach this equation from the other side, to attempt to take someone else into your hands, a reader about whom you know nothing: a stranger you're cruising. Like all writers and cruisers, I want to do something with you, or to you, or maybe to myself in front of you. But as with good sex, compatibility is required. On Grindr, you begin to figure this out by asking each new sexual prospect the same question, shortened to a single word: *Into?*

1

The Defense Rests

I'm driving on the interstate, on my way to teach. I've got some time to spare, though, so I exit the highway and pull into the parking lot of a rest area, glancing into the windows of parked cars as I pass them. Anybody home? Some windows are tinted opaque, which gets my imagination going. I choose a parking spot close to the restrooms: a good vantage point to surveil the scene.

Rest areas are designed for stopping on the way from somewhere to somewhere else. Some have gas stations and fast food. Others—like this one—have small, state-run canteens with restrooms, maps, tourist brochures, and vending machines. And some just have portable toilets and a few picnic tables. Most people stop here to empty their bladders or bowels, stretch their legs, or eat lunch, but I'm not here to rest, I'm here for quick, anonymous sex in the restroom.

After I park, I look back and forth between my rear and side mirrors, watching the lot. There are four or five other people also sitting alone in their idling cars, and also, I suspect, here for sex. But minutes pass and nobody moves, nothing happens. Despite the stillness, I feel anxious, on edge, *restless*. What if one of these guys is a cop? What if they're all cops? A few weeks ago, I was here late in the afternoon and the situation was similar: four or five people sitting in their cars. At five o'clock on the dot, everyone but me drove off, one after another in a procession. This would be a normal time to leave if you didn't want to explain to your wife, for example, why you were late coming home from work, but I grew paranoid, convinced that it was some kind of sting operation. What's worse, I bet that police departments send their hunkiest officers to entrap unwitting perverts; at a place like this, the hotter a guy is, the less I trust him. I read online that you should ask a guy to kiss you first if you think he might be a cop, because cops won't kiss. (I do know a guy who had sex at a rest area with an off-duty cop, but that's a different story.) What would I do if I were arrested? How poorly would I be treated at the precinct? I imagine my students sitting in our classroom, waiting, wondering what happened to me.

This is not the only thing that worries me. I also consider the possibility that I'll mistake someone's interest, that I'll solicit a guy and he'll be disgusted, enraged, violent. Or what if I'm hooking up with someone and we get caught in the act by a janitor or a random stranger? Would they attempt to detain us while calling the police? Would I run if they didn't? Would I deny any wrongdoing? In truth, even the prospect of a straightforward sexual encounter in a public restroom with no trouble whatsoever makes my palms sweat and my heart race.

Sitting alone in my parked car should be boring, but instead I feel like I'm preparing myself for a jump scare in a horror movie, watching the other cars intently, afraid that I'll be caught off guard if I look away. I realize that I'm literally holding my breath, trying to be completely silent. I really don't want to be the first one to make a move—to be seen and possibly pursued by men whose attractiveness I have not yet ascertained—but the tension is more than I can bear, and besides, I don't have all day, so I get out of my car, walk over to the building, and head inside.

č

A few years ago, I started to realize just how many public restrooms in my corner of the US are not only homoerotic—an uncomfortable truth given their stated purpose—but also horny. For most of my life, I was oblivious to this fact.

Freud writes that "the excremental is all too intimately and inseparably bound up with the sexual; the position of the genitals—*inter urinas et faeces*—is the decisive and unchangeable factor."[1] So too with public restrooms. I'm not talking about urophilia or coprophilia, though Freud might go there. I'm talking about the opportunities created by the urinal—to see and be seen—and by the stall—for anonymous contact.

Lee Edelman argues that public restrooms participate in the production of heterosexual subjects by segregating genders; each gender gets its own restroom, or rather, each restroom creates its own gender.[2] This production also happens through the differentiation of zones within the men's room; some zones are more private than others. In most men's rooms, urinals are more public, particularly in the absence of dividers, while stalls are more private. Edelman argues that this differentiation serves a purpose: the penis is displayed because penises should inspire pride, even when flaccid, unlike the anus, which should be hidden, especially while it is being pleasurably stimulated during defecation. At the same time, the proudly displayed penis must not be looked at by other men; it must not elicit sexual curiosity or desire. For this reason, it is acceptable, even important to monitor the gaze of other men at the urinal. In other words, don't look at other men's penises, but do try to verify that they're not looking at yours.

It is not lost on Edelman that this can easily backfire, which is how public restrooms became a popular site for sex between men in the first place, what with all those dicks being brandished without shame. Furthermore, the norms of propriety and etiquette that attempt to control restroom behavior are precisely what eroticizes transgression. Rules are what produce the thrill of breaking rules, of doing what must not be done.

I'm relieved to discover that the restroom is empty. It smells strongly of bleach, which is the best-case scenario. There are six or seven metal stalls against one wall and, opposite these, five urinals with no dividers between them. I strategically choose the urinal farthest and least visible from the entrance. I unzip my fly, take out my dick and hold it, pretending to pee. This feels awkward, but I prefer it to standing at the sink and washing my hands or fixing my appearance. Nothing says "inconspicuous men's room patron" like primping in the mirror for twenty minutes.

Norms prohibit me from looking around, so I rely on my hearing for cues. The white noise from the ventilation system in the restroom is loud, and I have to strain to listen. I hear the canteen door open, footsteps approaching, and then nothing; someone using the women's restroom, probably. Two minutes pass with only white noise and, below this, barely audible, a radio from a nearby office, where an attendant is stationed. I hear a toilet flush through the wall, then what sounds like a leaf blower (but is just a hand dryer) and footsteps receding. I hear the door open again and more footsteps approaching; whoever just left the building probably held the door open for someone else walking in. There is no door to the men's restroom—it's around a corner—which means no unsanitary door handles, but also no audible warning when someone new walks in. The footsteps get louder and then someone enters the restroom and my anxiety returns. I try to calm myself down so that I don't start to quiver—a weird and off-putting symptom of my excitement.

Using my peripheral vision, I try to figure out where this guy is going: stall or urinal, near or far. I'm pretty sure he's standing at the urinal farthest from me, which is common men's room etiquette, but doesn't necessarily mean that he's not cruising. I have no clue what he looks like. I listen for the sound of urine hitting porcelain. Five seconds, ten seconds, nothing. Is he listening too? Does he think I'm pee shy or that I have some kind of bladder issue? Should I send some kind of signal? I'm psyching myself up to glance ever so slightly in his direction when I hear the canteen door open again, footsteps, and then another guy walks into the restroom.

Continuing to use my peripheral vision, I see that the new guy has chosen the middle urinal—this is also common etiquette, though some guys will opt for a stall. I wonder: Is this about to be a circle jerk? Then I hear the faraway guy start to pee, or at least I think it's him. I wonder what took him so long. Maybe it's a prostate thing. I'm glad I didn't signal my interest. I can't tell whether the middle guy is peeing or not.

The faraway guy finishes, zips up, washes his hands, and leaves. It's just me, Middle, and the white noise now. Neither of us is audibly peeing. We are still, frozen in place, a staring contest with no eye contact. A minute goes by like this, though it feels like five. Every second that passes seems to confirm what's happening here, what's going to happen. The prospect of his desire excites me, though I still don't know what he looks like. What am I waiting for? I am as certain as I can be in this situation, and there isn't going to be a better moment, so I gather the courage to turn my head, and he meets my gaze.

My family lived in the Bronx until 1988, the year I turned ten. We lived off of Mosholu Parkway, a block from the last stop on the D train, and a fifteen-minute walk to the New York Botanical Garden. I went to the gardens a lot with my two older sisters. We'd sneak in through a hole in the chain link fence, which we'd discovered in a secluded, wooded part of the property. We once stumbled upon a man jerking off in the forest there. Did I understand what he was doing? Was I afraid? Excited? Was he really wearing a trench coat, or did my imagination furnish this cartoonish detail after the fact? How long did we allow ourselves to gawk at him before we ran off?

It only occurs to me now that this could have been a place where men went to cruise, that the hole in the fence hadn't been cut by garden enthusiasts too poor to afford the entrance fee. Sometimes my sisters and I would find condoms or their wrappers on the ground. I knew what condoms were, but had assumed—as I'd been taught—that they were used only to prevent pregnancy. My mom had a coworker at the time who was HIV-positive, which she'd told us matter-of-factly and without judgment. He'd contracted the virus by having sex with men, she said. Condoms weren't a part of the story. An article in the journal *AIDS Care* reports that 78 percent of gay and bisexual men used condoms by 1987 (versus 10 percent before 1980).[3]

When I was ten, we moved to a suburb in New Jersey. There were woods behind our new house, but no fence, no strange men, and no condoms—only skunk cabbage and the initials of bored teenagers carved into trees. I wonder where men went to cruise. There's a rest area on the Garden State Parkway in Montvale, not far from my town.

Middle is moving his forearm slowly, in an unmistakably masturbatory back-and-forth motion. I attempt a reciprocal kind of movement to make it clear that we're on the same page. We both back up a few inches, giving the other a better view. He's got a nice dick, smooth and uncut, average length and pleasantly thick. I still feel somewhat on edge, but my appetite is now louder than my anxiety. "This," I say to myself, "is how you get into trouble."

I spot a ring on the hand he's jerking off with, and I let myself believe that it's a wedding ring, willfully ignoring the hand and finger it's on. I like to think that many of the guys who hook up in public restrooms are married to women. As one guy put it to the queer writer Patrick Califia-Rice, "You know what I've learned in the toilets? I've learned that there's no such thing as a heterosexual. They can all be had."[4] Freud essentially says as much, proposing that humans are constitutionally bisexual. Writer and ex–porn star Conner Habib tells a story about having sex at a rest area with a guy who, after the deed was done, walked back to his car where his kids were waiting.[5] What a score.

I steal another glance at Middle's face. He looks to me to be Latinx, with a tidy gray beard and delicate, boyish features. I find the contrast attractive. There's still an empty urinal between us. Since we're alone for what might only be a moment, I step next to him. This emboldens him, and he reaches over and takes my hard dick in his hand. Then he leans over and whispers, "I've got a van," as if this weren't something a serial killer might say. I don't remember seeing a van in the parking lot, and I pretend not to hear him.

I'm surprised and turned on by how gently he holds me; some guys grab and yank like they're trying to open a stuck drawer. I can tell that this won't take long, for me at least. All the pieces have fallen into place—the scene, the guy, the act—each amplifying the other into a chain reaction over which I have little control. It only takes a few seconds of his light grip for me to finish. "Fuck yeah," he whispers, continuing to hold me as he picks up the pace on himself, whether because my orgasm turns him on, or because the likelihood of interruption increases over time, or because he knows that I've got a foot out the door at this point.

It does seem rude to leave immediately, and I'm curious about his orgasm, so I linger, my dick softening in his right hand while he masturbates feverishly with his left. There is a kind of desperation in his speed that I find unattractive now that I'm done. I know that this is not generous, and likely an expression of discomfort with my own feelings of excitement, but in less than a minute I want to go.

As luck would have it, we hear footsteps approaching, and my companion quickly withdraws his hand and leans forward into his urinal. This is an inopportune moment for him to pause, but a good one for me to zip up and exit, which I do, pausing briefly to wash my hands at the sink before walking back to my car, getting back on the highway, and driving to class.

Half a century after Stonewall, cruising is still widely understood to be disgraceful, gross, unhealthy, sick, and/or immoral, not to mention dangerous.[6] Societies pathologize sex like this in an attempt to control it with judgment and punishment. They ask, "What do you have to say for yourself, pervert?" but they don't really want to know; they just want contrition and penance.

In queer scholarship, there are two primary responses to the pathologization of queer sex. The first response is encapsulated in the essay "Thinking Sex" by Gayle Rubin, who takes a defensive approach, advocating for the destigmatization of homosexuality, cruising, BDSM, sex work, and the like.[7] As long as sex is consensual, she argues, why not let a million flowers bloom? According to Rubin, the policing of non-normative sex is essentially unwarranted: there is no real threat or danger in our sexual variation, just misplaced anxiety. As she puts it, sexual variation is "benign." She urges us all to be more like anthropologists, who "cherish different cultures as unique expressions of human inventiveness rather than as the inferior or disgusting habits of savages."[8] Rubin is, in other words, a sexual pluralist. If you don't like this or that kind of sex, by all means don't partake, but also don't try to stop other people from getting off, even if they're doing it in public.

Many queer scholars have taken a similarly defensive approach, arguing that there is nothing to fear in pathologized kinds of sex. There may even be something to embrace, in line with prevailing values. For example, Samuel Delany argues that the interracial and interclass contact that occurs in cruising spots is nothing short of a renewal of the public sphere.[9] As he writes,

> Contact is the conversation that starts in line at the grocery counter with the person behind you while the clerk is changing the paper roll in the cash register. It is the pleasantries exchanged with a neighbor who has brought her chair out to take some air on the stoop. It is the discussion that begins with the person next to you at a bar. It can be the conversation that starts with any number of semiofficial or service persons—mailmen, policemen, librarian, store clerk or counter person. As well, it can be two men watching each other masturbating together in adjacent urinals of a public john—an encounter that, later, may or may not become a conversation.

For Delany, fucking strangers isn't just a pleasurable convenience; it can help dismantle the segregation that structures social life.[10] According to this account, a white guy like me jerking off with a Latinx guy at a rest area isn't pathological, it's practically a civic duty. If gay men are stereotypically bad at intimacy, at least we're doing our part to strengthen the social fabric of the nation, albeit inadvertently. This appeal to politics is now well rehearsed in queer studies.[11]

A defensive posture is understandable; it's hard not to be defensive when you are under attack. As David M. Halperin succinctly puts it, "The world is waging a war on sex."[12] In the face of anti-queer bigotry, scholars like Rubin and Delaney look to politics for their defense. (It's more difficult—though not impossible—for queers to use nature or scripture to justify our existence like heterosexuals do.) It seems that it's not enough simply to say, "Leave us alone"; queers have to say, "Leave us alone because we're not hurting anyone" or "Leave us alone because we're solving intergroup conflict." Queer sex is judged according to whom and what it hurts or helps.

Like most queer people, I do want homophobes to leave me alone. I don't want to worry about getting gay-bashed or arrested in a public restroom. But I'm also not interested in defending myself or my fellow perverts from ridicule, discrimination, or persecution. I will not beg squeamish conservatives—or liberals, for that matter—to tolerate my desires and pleasures on the grounds that they're socially benign, politically salutary, psychologically therapeutic, or whatever. (On this score I do envy the free pass given to heterosexuals—who are never asked to justify their "orientation"—though I'm not envious enough to convert.) I understand, strategically speaking, why so much queer ink has been spilled to prove that our perversions are, at the very least, harmless. I am familiar with the bullshit and abuse to which queer people are routinely if unevenly subjected, and I'm sympathetic to the desire to disarm homophobes and eliminate sexual shame. The problem is that defending queer desires and pleasures has a cost: It cedes a lot of power to the intolerant, allowing them to set the terms of conversation, catering to their values and appeasing their demands for explanation, justification, reassurance, and apology. Confusing scholarship with activism, defense limits the kinds of questions one can ask, the kinds of things one can see, think, and say.[13] Everything gets filtered through the motive of defense, shrinking the imagination. It's also exhausting. This is a cost I'm unwilling to pay; the defense rests.[14]

℃

The second kind response to the pathologization of queer sex is exemplified by the essay "Is the Rectum a Grave?" by Leo Bersani. Responding to the rage and violence directed at gay men during the AIDS crisis of the

1980s, Bersani proposes that homophobia is motivated by a rejection of male bottoming. He argues that bottoming is not a benign sexual variation (as Rubin would have it), but rather strikes at the heart of male identity because it turns a man into a promiscuous woman, figuratively speaking. In so doing, bottoming represents a threat to patriarchy, a system of male (over)empowerment. According to this idea, homophobes are invested in sadistic, phallic power, and they correctly recognize bottoming as a threat. Needless to say, Bersani is critical of patriarchy, and he is interested in bottoming precisely because of its transgressive qualities. I'm inclined to overextend and literalize his argument as suggesting that the solution to homophobia isn't tolerance, as Rubin argues, but rather for homophobic men to lie on their backs, spread their legs, and open wide, finally getting in touch with their disavowed masochism. Of course, given the sex scandals that some homophobic conservatives find themselves embroiled in, one might justifiably conclude that they are indeed aware of the pleasures of bottoming and of the threat that bottoming represents to their particular brand of masculinity.

If Rubin is a sexual pluralist, Bersani is closer to a sexual evangelist. Unlike Rubin, he makes no attempt to reassure or even speak to the intolerant; Bersani is interested in homophobes only insofar as their horror and disgust inadvertently reveal the revolutionary potential of bottoming. He suggests that there is, in fact, something dangerous about particular kinds of sex, and that this "something" is what makes them useful, politically speaking. How can something as mundane as sex be so revolutionary? Bersani imagines a link between how we have sex and how society is organized, the former shaping the latter—an intriguing reversal of the more common proposition that social norms shape our sexual desires. As Michel Foucault (from whom Bersani draws) puts it: "We have to understand that with our desires, through our desires, go new forms of relationships, new forms of love, new forms of creation. Sex is not a fatality: it's a possibility for creative life."[15]

Scholars (including Bersani himself) have elaborated and challenged the provocations in "Rectum" in various compelling ways.[16] Yet I'm still drawn to its evangelism, its resolute refusal to pacify bigots, and its identification of the revolutionary value of a man who relishes being penetrated. It shouldn't be surprising that those of us who have been treated like villains because of our desires and pleasures might enjoy reimagining ourselves as heroes of a sort. Instead of saying, "We (gay men) are harmless," as Rubin does, Bersani says something more like, "We're a threat to patriarchy." This rejection of the desirability of heterosexuality appeals to me politically—as a way of contesting the heteronormative assumption that nobody would choose to be gay. I know that Bersani's argument is anti-identitarian, which would preclude any kind of group-based pride, but I nonetheless find it appealing, in part, in identitarian terms. Let heterosexuals be the ones to ask for tolerance and forgiveness from gay people, to reassure and explain to us how their sexual desires and pleasures have nothing to do with their long history of violence. I'm being vengeful, but Bersani's approach isn't about vengeance, it's strategic. Like Rubin, he wants to rid the world of sadistic violence, but he doesn't think that tolerance will work; quite the opposite. His argument isn't just about undoing homophobia, it's about undoing men. As Tom Roach puts it, in slightly different terms, "At this historical juncture, normatively socialized American men are arguably most in need of learning fungibility's lessons"—some men more than others.[17]

Bersani is hardly alone in identifying a higher purpose for sex. In addition to Delany, for whom cruising serves an important democratic function, Bersani is joined by scholars and activists on the left like Catharine MacKinnon and Andrea Dworkin, who spearheaded the feminist campaign against pornography (sex should advance gender equality); Adrienne Rich and Ti-Grace Atkinson, the latter of whom famously declared that "feminism was the theory, lesbianism the practice" (sex should dismantle patriarchy); Ellen Willis, who championed the cause of women's sexual pleasure (sex should undermine authoritarianism); Amia Srinivasan, who inherits Willis's allergy to moralism, but also her morally inflected political commitments (sex should promote social equality in general); and Avgi Saketopoulou, who embraces the "generative potential" of perversity (sex should be therapeutic).[18] Then there are the conservatives, who similarly imbue sex with purpose, albeit religious, heteropatriarchal, or ethno-nationalist. And while there is endless disagreement between the left and the right—and between near neighbors on the left, as Willis pointed out forty years ago—about what the purpose of sex should be, it is the shared belief that sex needs to serve a higher purpose that makes disagreement possible. Left or right, liberal or progressive, sex-positive or Victorian, nearly everyone seems to agree that sex should be redemptive: politically, ethically, socially, psychologically, or spiritually.

Even Edelman—who rejects the idea that queerness is an "oppositional political identity" rather than an "opposition to politics"—still assigns a political role to queers, as when he asserts that queers "must respond" to homophobia by repudiating that which fuels our oppression: "the social order and the Child in whose name we're collectively terrorized; . . . Laws both with capital Ls and with small; . . . [and] the whole network of Symbolic relations and the future that serves as its prop."[19] My interest in thinking about sex without sublimating its pleasure to a higher purpose owes much to Edelman's unwillingness to redeem queerness; unwilling because he knows that what we do "in the bed or the bar or the baths" is fundamentally incompatible with collective politics and the society it organizes.[20] And while I am certainly sympathetic to "resisting enslavement to the future in the name of having a life"—indeed, I'm arguing here that my (sex) life requires no justification—Edelman's language of choosing, resisting, and insisting, even "intransitively," remains tied to its foe.[21] It's not that I disagree with him, it's that I want to think about sex without focusing on those who want to destroy us, and what if anything we the perverts can do about it, urgent though this question may be.

The left's uneasiness with pleasure is hardly new. In the 1930s, the Marxist cultural critic Theodor Adorno sought to understand why the exploited and alienated masses hadn't revolted against capitalism. His explanation: their insatiable appetite for inane trinkets and ditties, which kept them temporarily, superficially satisfied and made them stupid and docile.[22] Before Adorno, Marx himself famously took issue with opioids, metaphorically speaking. How frustrating this must have been for Adorno, watching the wretched of the earth refuse to claim their rightful throne and liberate all of humanity from the shackles of capitalism, and for what: the jitterbug?

If pleasure is a problem for many on the left, this is not simply because hedonism forestalls revolution, but because pleasure is characteristically self-indulgent, irresponsible, and antisocial, particularly in the absence of moderation; and many on the left are deeply committed to altruism, responsibility, and the social. This is not to say that pleasure is strictly a solo affair; as Kane Race argues (via Foucault and Howard Becker), "New techniques and procedures [of pleasure] are acquired" from others.[23] Rather, it is to point out that in a state of pleasure, one risks losing sight of other people and their needs and desires. As Delany explains (of his uncle's homophobia), "What homosexuality and prostitution represented . . . was the untrammeled pursuit of pleasure; and the untrammeled pursuit of pleasure was the opposite of social responsibility."[24] It is considered selfish to pursue your own pleasure with little regard to others' welfare, and the more privilege you have, the more ethically dubious this pursuit. To make matters worse, pleasure sells itself. People may need some instruction when it comes to learning how to enjoy something new, but they generally don't need to be persuaded to pursue pleasure; its appeal is self-evident, even for puritans, maybe especially for them. It is society that needs to be made desirable, with all of its requirements, regulations, impositions, and sanctions.

One way that some on the left have attempted to make the social more palatable is by emphasizing the cooperative nature of particular pleasures—team sports, community gardening, campfire singalongs—thereby downplaying the tension between pleasure and responsibility.[25] And then there's the pleasure (or satisfaction) of helping: of setting aside individualistic pleasures in order to care for others—or convincing ourselves that this is what we're doing.[26] This is the "pleasure" of being good. More individualistic pleasures might still be ethically salvageable when successfully narrated as "self-care" and justified in relation to one's group-based oppression ("Caring for myself is not self-indulgence, it is self-preservation, and that is an act of political warfare") or as nurturing our interdependency ("When I take care of myself, I often am also taking care of others").[27] And if that seems too far-fetched, embracing moderation might help. It is possible, after all, to work hard and play hard; some of the most fun people I know are committed activists, which is not to say that most of the committed activists I know are fun people.

These discursive maneuvers might provide some comfort to those anxious about the siren song of hedonism, but they avoid the heart of the matter. As long as the left prioritizes ethics, pleasure will be a problem. Even among the more liberationist factions of the left—for example, sex-positive feminists like Willis—there is often an ethical bottom line, which can't help but renounce the pursuit of pleasure and declare fealty to the social. The requirement that sex be ethical is not only limiting (in terms of how we talk about sex); it's also moralizing: valuing some desires and pleasures and pathologizing others. Even when this valuing is a response to others' intolerance, it nonetheless does what all valuing does: promising reward for whatever is deemed good and punishment for whatever is deemed bad, effectively coercing behavior while also potentially (and ironically) making the forbidden more desirable.

Just as I'm not interested in defending my desires and pleasures against pearl-clutching homophobes, I'm also not interested in defending them against finger-wagging socialists, ethical sluts, or virtuous queers. In addition to being limiting, defending myself suggests a kind of certainty about sex that feels disingenuous to me. Inspired by the nonjudgmental introspection of scholars and writers like Maggie Nelson and Michelle Tea, I feel more curious than I do certain, frustrating as this might be for inquisitors who want a confession, contrition, and penance. In this spirit, I'd like to replace talk of values and principles with talk of desires and pleasures; "What do you care about?" is a different question than "What turns you on?"

As for the rare thinkers on the left (like Bersani) who offer politics without ethics—just straight-up self-advocacy—sex is still valued for its utility. Of course, there are important differences between attacking pleasure (like Adorno), defending pleasure (like Rubin and Delaney), and nondefensively asserting the utility of pleasure (like Bersani), but these differences concern which cause pleasure should serve and how, not the basic proposition that it should serve some cause in the first place. It is remarkable that even on the queer left, the indulgence of pleasure so often requires justification.

It is certainly possible that sex might do (or undo) some of the things that the left wants it to, but it shouldn't have to. Sex shouldn't have to make us healthier, happier, or more peaceful, equal, autonomous, or free. It shouldn't have to heal us—or be "psychically useful," as Tim Dean puts it—or bring us together.[28] It shouldn't have to answer to others' moral, aesthetic, political, or religious disapproval.[29] When we talk about sex, we shouldn't have to demonstrate our commitment to the struggle, or placate bigots by proving that queers aren't sick, evil sociopaths, or reassure ourselves that we're not bad people (or not worse than anyone else, at least). As Dean and Oliver Davis write, "Today we want so much from sex—as if we believed that economic inequalities and their social consequences could somehow be remedied, or compensated, by achieving equality between sexual partners, equality between genders, or the equal distribution of pleasure in erotic experience. Our culture has massively overburdened sexual intercourse with expectation and freighted it with significance, including political significance."[30] Few on the left, it seems, are willing to just let sex be.[31] Sex doesn't need a higher purpose, and pleasure shouldn't be a problem; in fact, it might be the very point, or at least one point. "It's my pleasure" should be justification enough. To reiterate Rubin's point while not putting it in the service of a larger sociopolitical goal: As long as sex is consensual, why not let a million flowers bloom?[32]

I am intimately familiar with the inclination to find the messianic within the mundane. I was a "red diaper baby": In the 1970s, my parents were members of the Revolutionary Communist Party, and they treated labor with a respect that bordered on reverence. They held no illusions about labor under capitalism—they understood that in most places, most of the time, working conditions are substandard if not appalling. But they also believed that under radically different political-economic conditions (i.e., the control of the proletariat), labor could be liberatory: no exploitation or alienation, just the life-affirming wholesomeness of willingly sacrificing one's time and energy for the collective good, even if it still involved, for example, emptying hospital bedpans (my father was briefly an orderly, a job he acquired for the purpose of unionizing other employees).

My sisters and I were raised in this faith. Our parents routinely hauled us to political demonstrations: no blood for oil, US out of Nicaragua, no justice, no peace. We were on the side of workers and of the social groups oppressed and exploited to further capitalists' interests: Black and brown people, immigrants, women, the poor. When I was ten years old, I started attending a secular Jewish, socialist sleepaway summer camp in western Massachusetts—Camp Kinderland—where kids learned about social justice, painted murals to honor various struggles for liberation around the world, mourned those killed by war and genocide, and every day after lunch distributed candy mailed by parents (called "kassa," Yiddish for treasure) equally among everyone in each bunk. Picture a group of disheveled tweens sitting in a circle in the grass and singing, with uneven enthusiasm, the anticolonial Puerto Rican anthem "Que Bonita Bandera," lead by a tough, Yiddish-speaking grandmother from the Bronx. That was Kinderland.

Kinderland's "cultural program," as it was called (somewhat sinisterly, I now think), was not so important to me, though it was connected to a general spirit of kindness that was a welcome reprieve from social exclusion and bullying at school. Kinderland was also a place where I fooled around sexually with some of the boys in my bunk; the heteronormativity of this little leftist enclave was not without its advantages. I was a legibly gay child under the care of camp counselors and administrators who welcomed gayness in theory but were unwilling or unable to address it in practice, which included coming-of-age staples like mutual masturbation after lights out. The formal prohibition of sex between campers at

Kinderland—justified, as I recall, by the lack of privacy (as if this weren't a turn-on)—was an early lesson for me in the tension between community and sexuality, rules and desires, justice and freedom, being good and feeling good. During the day, I paid a lot of lip service to the party line (community, rules, justice, being good), while at night I voted with my feet (sexuality, desires, freedom, feeling good).

I wasn't raised entirely in a far-left bubble. When I was ten years old—the age I started going to Kinderland—my family moved to a middle-class New Jersey town where centrist Democrat was as far left as it got, where we had to stand for the Pledge of Allegiance at school each morning, and where I was called faggot and pussy by guys whose masculinity—established, in part, at my expense—earned them prime billing in my nascent sexual fantasies. (If I was going to suffer, why not get something out of it?) Not only was I gay, I was hot for my bullies.

The idiosyncratic politics I inherited from my parents became a central facet of my adolescent identity. I was not only different from my Jersey peers, but better, more enlightened, or so I told myself. (If I was going to be alienated, why not do it on my own terms?) I knew that there were other places—like Kinderland—where I fit in, places more interesting than Hillsdale and more suitable for a sophisticate like me. (I was also a snob.) Never mind that I was too shy to be an activist, too lazy to work for free, and too superficial to disavow the pleasures of consumer culture. I was a closeted gay boy and a closeted hedonist.

When I arrived at NYU as an undergrad, I sought out the left I already knew, collecting a handful of Marxist professors who rewarded my ability to rehearse the ideology and didn't challenge—or seem to notice—my disinterest in community organizing, let alone interacting with any actual proletarians, whoever and wherever they were (factories?). My favorite professors were like that: well-versed in left political thought and, as far as I could tell, not much else, which was fine with me. The closest I came to legible activism was when I was arrested at the Critical Mass RNC protest in Manhattan in 2004, and that was a total surprise.

I'm reminded of Andrea Long Chu's characterization of feminism on the internet as "a form of generating feelings of belonging that uses forms of knowledge, not insofar as they are true or false, but insofar as they help produce a feeling of being with others."[33] My parents' politics did this for me, giving me a feeling of belonging when I desperately wanted one. Over time, this yearning to belong was mitigated by an allergy to social regulation; belonging, I learned, was rarely without cost.

In college, ethically grounded politics supplied me with a robust intellectual foundation. I processed everything through my socialism: "Is it good for the workers?" This gave me a clear sense of right and wrong that allowed me to form opinions and cast judgments. I defended my ideas and taste as politically righteous no matter what, which made me a resourceful thinker, if not a particularly smart one As Torrey Peters writes, "A nimble mind can always uncover the politics to justify its own selfishness."[34] If I didn't like something, I dismissed it with contempt as conservative or reactionary. If not for my goofy, non-masculine demeanor, I would have been totally insufferable.

These politics also gave purpose to my thinking and writing. I have Marx's eleventh thesis on Feuerbach committed to memory, thanks to my father: "The philosophers have only interpreted the world, in various ways; the point is to change it."[35] Why write anything, I wondered, if not to further some political project. As Chu observes:

> There are these disciplines which are founded on the idea that doing academic work is a form of political action. This is the fantasy of critique as a political act. When I say fantasy I don't mean something that isn't true, I just mean something which you would believe *even if it wasn't true*. And what this fantasy means is that we often tend to do one of two things when we look at objects: we either bludgeon them for being too complicit with the status quo, or we celebrate them for reflecting membership in the very same political project in which we as critics believe that we are, *in this moment*, in the writing of criticism, participating. So what that means is that we spend a lot of time looking for objects in which we can see our own reflections and not a lot of time sitting with objects that disappoint us.[36]

I'm reminded of the hundreds of articles, essays, and books I've read that happen to find good politics in whatever thing the author already enjoys. How convenient that one's politics should align with one's desires.[37] It is worth wondering, as Jack Halberstam asks, "why we cannot tolerate the linking of our desires to politics that disturb us."[38]

I understand the appeal of concluding, as if after dispassionate consideration, that whatever you already enjoy or desire—or dislike—happens to make you a good person, or that it serves some higher purpose: justice, equality, peace, self-actualization, enlightenment. I'm hardly immune to this temptation. I'm also intimately familiar with those for whom discipline and a higher purpose—and, perhaps, the supreme thrill of transgression—are themselves the primary objects of desire: the materialists who reject shopping, the Catholics who won't masturbate, the men who swear off pornography, the heterosexual women who refuse the company of men, all in the name of salvation or revolution and the moral clarity they promise. But this now feels unsatisfying to me. I want to think and write without a political or ethical motive. Politics gave me purpose, perspective, and identity. It helped to armor my psyche against homophobes, to develop compassion for other people who are treated poorly, and to access social currency at Kinderland, NYU, and CUNY (where I went to grad school). And it sensitized me to the social organization of power. But it also stifled my curiosity, inhibited my ability to apprehend complexity, and—through shaming moralism—made it difficult to acknowledge and examine desires that would have made me a bad person. Perry Zurn argues that curiosity is inherently political—on the side of "conquest, sovereignty, patriarchy, marginalization" but also "dissent, counterinformation, resistance movements, and social justice"—but this kind of insistence on the political (which is also a mandate) can ironically suppress forms of curiosity that lead elsewhere.[39]

I can't deny that I'm intrigued by other people's judgments, but having to answer to them gets old. I'm not interested in defending or valuing my sex; I'm interested in thinking in modes other than defense or valuation—to examine, wonder, and speculate—while ignoring those who demand judgment: good or bad, benign or malignant, therapeutic or pathological, revolutionary or regressive.[40] When you are forced to justify sex, it becomes hard to really look at it, to sit with it. When the stakes are high, a certain kind of story must be told. It is liberating to let this requirement go, to stop worrying about whether or not I will be found righteous or wicked (and be rewarded or punished for it), whether or not I will inadvertently give fodder to homophobes or otherwise set the cause back. When I stop worrying about these things, it becomes easier to peer at the unsavory, or more to the point, to suspend judgments like "unsavory" and indulge my curiosity, to marvel—as Rubin does—at sexual variation. As it turns out, I may be more of a pluralist than an evangelist, not because I want to disarm homophobes, but because I want to disregard them.

Rest area sex was a revelation to me. Among other things, it changed how I experience these places. They feel different now, tinged with lust and vice, even when I'm only stopping to pee. The pleasure of sociology, as Peter Berger describes it, lies in witnessing the familiar transform into the strange, and that's how it felt watching bathrooms turn into bathhouses once I knew where to look, how to stand and sit, and when to make a move.[41]

Of course, when you're queer, the familiar may already be strange, and to make it strange in a different way may effectively make it more familiar, as Sara Ahmed observes.[42] For example, I'd long felt awkward using public restrooms for their stated purpose, because I feared that I'd somehow inadvertently expose my desire. But as these spaces became queer to me, I started to feel more comfortable in them, empowered even, if not exactly relaxed. Lingering in rest areas, watching people come and go, identifying cruisers and having sex with some of them, and occasionally making small talk with custodians all helped me to feel like these places exist for me and my purpose as much as they do for anyone else. As Shaka McGlotten writes, "Every space might become a queer space, if only I paid attention to sometimes faint but almost always present erotic frequencies."[43]

Nonetheless, in places where public sex is illegal and queerness is pathologized, cruisers risk assault, arrest, and worse. This risk varies depending on cruisers' social locations and circumstances.[44] Suffice it to say, for those of us who cruise, the pleasure outweighs the risk. And for some of us, the risk enhances the pleasure. While I'm hardly sympathetic to the police officers who entrap cruisers, I wonder what they too might be risking, psychically speaking, when they join the game.[45]

People have different tolerances for risk and are differently exposed to risk, but we all need some risk in our sex lives, as psychotherapist Esther Perel argues.[46] For better or worse, sex is a characteristically risky undertaking. In sex, we risk a lot: rejection; failing to satisfy or be satisfied; failing to inhabit a particular desired gender position; feeling or causing pain, disappointment, regret, disgust, or embarrassment; misreading and miscommunicating; losing control over ourselves; and experiencing various kinds of injury. In addition to these risks—which can be amplified or muted in cruising—and the risk of interpersonal and institutional violence that cruisers face, many of us risk a deeper sense of safety and security that comes from knowing our sexual partners, or believing that we do. I explore this risk in the next chapter. One of the marvels of cruising is that it may not be much of a risk at all if it reliably pays off with pleasure.

2

Impersonal Intimacy

To celebrate my thirty-seventh birthday, I went to a Korean spa with a reputation for cruising. I'd never been to a Korean spa before, though there are a handful in the New York City area. I'd also never been to a bathhouse, gay or otherwise. I spent an hour meandering around the coed part of the facility while I worked up the courage to explore the gender-segregated "men's area"—a space adjacent to the locker room with several hot tubs, a sauna, and a steam room—where nudity is mandatory (hence the lively cruising). Back in the locker room, I took off my bathing suit and shirt, folded them neatly, and put them into my locker.

The transition to the men's area is not gradual. You open a glass door, and there you are with all the other naked men in a large windowless room. The management has done their best to class up the space with ocher walls and slate tiles on the floor, like the patio of a Tuscan villa reconstructed inside a shopping mall. My birthday fell on a weekend and it was crowded. Most guys seemed to be there alone, though a few were talking to a friend or boyfriend, or maybe someone they just met, their chatter barely audible above the white noise that fills the room—the combined sound of jacuzzi jets, people taking showers, and a powerful ventilation system.

I felt like an awkward teenager at first, holding the small, spa-provided towel in front of my crotch in a way that I hoped looked casual. I tried not to gawk at the array of diverse bodies on display; staring felt either impolite or too forward. But as time passed, I began to acclimate, feeling more at ease in my nakedness and more comfortable letting my gaze wander.

The vibe was sexually charged, but nothing illicit seemed to be going on in the sauna or steam room as far as I could tell. In the largest of the hot tubs, though, a group of men were sitting very close to each other without moving or speaking, their eyes lowered or closed. Above water their bodies were completely still. Below water everything was obscured by a blur of moving water and bubbles. What couldn't I see? I waited until a spot opened up in the hot tub and then I lowered myself in. After a few minutes I felt my neighbor's leg brush against my own and then pull away: an invitation, I suspected, with plausible deniability. I slowly moved my leg toward my neighbor and we touched again, more firmly this time, and held. He began to rub his leg gently against mine, while above water we sat like adjacent strangers on the subway. I didn't know what would happen next or what *could* happen given that any arm movement would be indiscreet. Then I felt something new on my leg—his foot—inching its way up.

Writing for the *New York Times* in 2016, Michael Musto pondered whether apps like Grindr were having a dampening effect on gay nightlife; why go out to eat when you can order in?[1] An earlier article in *New York Magazine* made a similar point about Fire Island's "meat rack"—a stretch of uninhabited forest famous for its uninhibited cruising.[2] Would Grindr effectively kill public sex?[3]

I agree with Musto that Grindr can feel convenient—sex on demand, when the stars align, at least for someone with my particular "stats" where I live. Grindr transforms the place of cruising—instead of meaningful glances in a public restroom, Grindr users exchange messages while sitting in bed, at our desks, on the bus, or standing in line. In this way, Grindr also transforms the time of cruising, extending it by imbuing mundane moments with the possibility of sex, mitigating the boredom of a commute, errands, familial obligations, or the workday.

For the same reason, though, cruising on Grindr can be tedious: I open the app, check my messages, maybe respond, see if anyone new has shown up, maybe write to them, close the app, wait a few minutes and repeat. And on and on and on.[4] Furthermore, as one of Shaka McGlotten's interviewees puts it, "You might be able to get dick to your house faster than a pizza, . . . but for many the dick might be late, it might ask for an exorbitant tip, or it might not be hot anymore when it did arrive."[5] Perhaps it took something like Grindr to highlight the particular affordances of in-person cruising for those of us late to the game.

Intrigued and turned on by the scene at the spa, I became a regular. I quickly learned that I prefer weekdays, which are less crowded. Unlike Grindr, cruising at the spa rarely feels tedious, because I don't have the time (or inclination) to spend all day, every day, hanging out. After racking up so many wasted hours on Grindr, this kind of restriction feels oddly innovative. At the spa, I arrive, relax for a while, and at some point I either find somebody I like (and who likes me), or I settle for somebody I like well enough, or I leave. The spa feels more limited, more of a gamble than Grindr, and more like a race against time. There are other regulars, of course, but you never know who else might unexpectedly show up.

In the hot tub, I can't always tell whether the person next to me wants to hook up—either in general, or with me. Sometimes I don't know who is next to me at all, if I don't catch a glimpse of their face or body. Feeling too awkward to crane my neck to look, my sense of them comes from our contact below, like an underwater glory hole.

> The glory hole is usually a circular opening, roughly 6–7 inches in diameter, cut into the wall at penis height between adjacent rooms. They can be found in bathhouses, saunas, and sometimes in adult video arcades, nightclubs, bookstores, sex shops, and between the stalls of public toilets known colloquially in the gay community as "cottages" or "tea rooms." Individuals on opposite sides of the wall have limited physical and visual contact with each other, while the hole allows direct contact with specific bodily organs that can be displayed through these openings and through which pleasure can be shared, bodily fluids exchanged.[6]

Sound risky? No guts, no glory.

There is something embarrassing about technical descriptions of deviant behavior written for the uninitiated—the awkward intersection of perversion and PowerPoint. See, for example, Laud Humphreys's canonical gay ethnography *Tearoom Trade*: "I believe ethnographic methods are the only truly empirical ones for the social scientist. When human behavior is being examined, systematic observation is essential; so I had to become a participant-observer of furtive, felonious acts."[7] Had to!

I often feel physically disoriented in the hot tub by the jets and bubbles and by the white noise that fills the room. Sometimes I can't tell where my body is or where other people's bodies are. I'll try stretching out horizontally and poking a toe above water to see where I end; like many men, I'm often a lot shorter than I think. I'll also try to position myself in such a way that makes discreet, accidental contact possible. The other person will also need to be carefully positioned; we might both reach out and still miss each other amid the aquatic turbulence. I'll wonder: Where are their legs? Are they sitting, crouching, kneeling? Am I reaching too far, or not far enough, or in the wrong direction? I'll aim for a particular part of their body and land elsewhere. I'll search for a landmark—knee, belly button—to get my bearings. Guys who look hung from far away can feel small in my hand. Hair and skin that looks coarse can feel soft. The jets are powerful, and it can be difficult to tell whether I'm being touched by another person or just by moving water. Away from the jets, my sense of touch is heightened; even the gentlest contact, if unexpected, is startling. Sometimes I'm annoyed by the bubbles—I just want to know where things are—but other times I appreciate them as a kind of clothing, a cover that makes it possible to explore and discover.

As a sighted and hearing person, touch can be an odd way to first experience somebody. Each guy touches me differently, and I think of them differently as a result. Some take their time, advancing and then withdrawing a knee for endless minutes. Other guys skip foreplay entirely. Their techniques differ. Some guys oscillate between tickling, groping, rubbing, and squeezing, varying the location, strength, and aggression of their touch. Others just grab and jerk the only way they seemingly know how. An underwater hand job can be unpleasant in the absence of a foreskin to reduce friction. Some guys understand this challenge, and others don't, or don't care.

Some guys seem to have a specific and unchanging set of desires, at least in relation to me. They want to be touched (or to touch me) in just one way, or not to be touched at all, and seem oblivious to feedback, or else uninterested in it. My own desire is more fluid. Or rather, I can be surprised by the pleasure of kinds of touch I don't specifically desire. I can't predict by scanning the room whose touch I might enjoy.[8] Being attractive is little indication. Maggie Nelson calls this "emergent desire."[9]

One difference between sight/hearing and touch is that sight/hearing can give you a sense of things at a distance, while touch only reports things that are proximate; when something is far away, you might be able to see/hear it, but not touch it. Despite this proximity, touch can be hazy. Something touches my leg: Is it an insect? A blade of grass? The wind? When I was ten years old, I was walking with my bike when I tripped and fell. My bike landed awkwardly on top of me. I stood up, picked up my bike, and resumed walking. Half a minute later my foot felt wet. I looked down and saw that one the bike's gears had cut my ankle in a series of parallel gashes; my foot was covered in blood. It looked serious but wasn't particularly painful. Still, I panicked, reacting to what I saw over what I felt (or didn't feel).

Like pain, pleasure can be hazy, diffuse, and hard to localize. It seems to emerge from points of contact—where someone or something touches your body—drawing attention to the surface of the body while also potentially producing the paradoxical sensation of an erasure of the body's surface.[10] This paradoxical sensation of surface/no surface can be felt intensely during sex, not simply because it sometimes involves penetration (a literal breach of the body's surface), but because of the way erotic contact can engender an existential kind of opening up, a shattering of subjectivity.[11] I wonder what else might be shattered or undone when our sense of self is pleasurably upended.[12]

Freud proposed that as infants we learn to experience external stimulation as pleasure; otherwise we'd be overwhelmed, undone by a flood of sensory input. It's ironic and fortunate that later in life we can take pleasure in self-shattering; rather than panicking, we can be turned on.[13]

I soon learned that more goes on at the spa—in the steam room, sauna, and restroom—but to take part I had to figure out how to signal my interest and availability discreetly.[14] There is a time and a place. As Tim Dean writes, "Public sex is not Dionysian, indiscriminate activity but carefully self-regulated and fully socialized behavior, with its own etiquette and conventions. Except for cruising in parks and on beaches, most public sex occurs in institutions that, by definition, are part of civilized society rather than an intrinsic threat to it."[15] Threat or no threat, there are conventions of behavior at the spa, and most guys follow them, with a few exceptions. Every so often a guy will walk from the hot tub to the steam room with a full erection, completely exposed, no towel. In the middle of a steam room circle jerk, this type of guy never seems to understand why everyone else rushes to hide their erections when someone new opens the door and walks in. There are also guys on the other end of the spectrum: too shy, nervous, or simply unaware of the posture and gestures required to signal interest. Most guys, though, are savvy enough to figure out the code, bold enough to make something happen when the moment is right, and discreet enough to avoid detection.

And then there are the guys who aren't cruising at all: bodybuilders stretching and soothing sore muscles, small groups of chatty friends, and guys clearing their sinuses, meditating, or dozing off. When many of these guys are around, the day can grow long with waiting, fingers and toes wrinkled from soaking, skin flushed from heat and itchy from chlorine.[16] Sometimes the offender is a single, solitary guy occupying a seat in the steam room for what feels like hours. Sometimes it's three or four men on rotation, sitting for ten or fifteen minutes at a time; when one finally gets up and leaves, another somehow materializes, as if on hetero community watch.

I'm not turned on by the presence of these other guys, but rather by the discretion necessitated by their presence; they might be offended—perhaps violently—by a sexual solicitation or by becoming unwitting bystanders to group sex. (I once walked into the steam room in the middle of a conflict between a cruiser and a man who'd been offended by whatever sexual activity or proposition had just transpired. "Live and let live," was the crux of the cruiser's impassioned defense.) This dynamic transforms relatively mundane and innocuous forms of contact—knees touching underwater—into something intensely erotic to me. I suspect that this has something to do with my childhood and adolescent sexual encounters, which often took place with unwitting adults, family members, or friends nearby, and therefore required discretion.

The risk of getting caught doesn't specifically excite me, though I do sometimes take pleasure in being looked at, watched, and admired by others. There is something titillating to me about the vulnerability of exposure—one reason to keep sex dirty, inappropriate, and shameful. If imposter syndrome is a kind of punishment for having been closeted for years, the erotic charge of exposure is a kind of consolation prize.

While I enjoy discreet, charged contact with guys in the men's area, a few hours of it is usually enough. After that, I'll want the cock blockers to leave so that I can get off and get on with my day. Why are they even here, I'll wonder in frustration, when there are women to be gawked at in the coed areas of the spa? Do they want to see how they measure up? Are they "naturists"? Do they come from other places with long-established cultures of naked men sweating and soaking together platonically? Do they bring friends with them to reduce the boredom of sitting around, or for "male bonding"? But even when I'm annoyed, there is something sweet to me about the idea that some of these guys know what's going on and don't mind, that they are indifferent to the rest of us getting off in their presence, or are even jealous of the ease with which we do it.

❡

The concept of intimacy is typically used to describe a kind of closeness that comes from knowing another person very well (and vice versa): their histories, deeply held secrets, innermost desires, most shameful pleasures, and hidden flaws.[17] Why do we want to know so much about other people? Is it human nature? Innocent curiosity? The way we were socialized? Is it an ethical impulse, as if it's a foregone conclusion that we will love and care for other people once they've been demystified to us, rather than being disappointed, displeased, or disgusted by them and abandoning them?

The desire to know other people, to forge intimacy with them, rarely elicits scrutiny because of its normativity in contemporary American culture. Particularly when it comes to sex, an intimate relationship is typically deemed to be a good relationship, or at least better than an impersonal relationship. Intimacy isn't just a quality that relationships can possess, it's a quality they should possess. It's not just something one might want, but something one should want, because it's natural, healthy, fulfilling, and important.

Just as intimacy is valued, impersonality is devalued. Well-adjusted adults are supposed to grapple with who their sexual partners really are—with all their faults, flaws, and weaknesses—never mind who they want them to be, or imagine them to be. This is how you build intimacy. As Jonathan Franzen put it in a commencement speech adapted for publication in the *New York Times*:

> The simple fact of the matter is that trying to be perfectly likable is incompatible with loving relationships. Sooner or later, for example, you're going to find yourself in a hideous, screaming fight, and you'll hear coming out of your mouth things that you yourself don't like at all, things that shatter your self-image as a fair, kind, cool, attractive, in-control, funny, likable person. Something realer than likability has come out in you, and suddenly you're having an actual life.[18]

A little later in the speech, Franzen qualifies this idea: "This is not to say that love is only about fighting. Love is about bottomless empathy, born out of the heart's revelation that another person is every bit as real as you are. And this is why love, as I understand it, is always specific. . . . To love a specific person, and to identify with his or her struggles and joys as if they were your own, you have to surrender some of your self." Franzen's target, in this speech, is our infatuation with our phones, devices, and screens. This infatuation, he argues, expresses "our fantasy ideal of an erotic relationship, in which the beloved object asks for nothing and gives everything, instantly, and makes us feel all powerful, and doesn't throw terrible scenes when it's replaced by an even sexier object and is consigned to a drawer." Unlike our devices, which seem to fulfill our desires easily and without complaint (according to Franzen), people are messy and ought to be considered as ends in and of themselves.

Disability activist Mia Mingus similarly proposes that "ugliness is a pathway to intimacy. You can't have intimacy without trust, and you can't have trust without vulnerability. In order to be vulnerable, you have to reveal parts of yourself that are capital-U Ugly."[19] I think I'd find these accounts of intimacy more compelling if they didn't make it sound like such a noble enterprise, as if the desire for closeness might not also be motivated by aggression or by feeling scared, trapped, or pathetic.

Evaluating the presence or absence of intimacy in casual, anonymous sex is thus a fraught exercise because there is a lot at stake; if cruising can be intimate, this means it can be good and therefore might not warrant pathologization.[20] As Shaka McGlotten writes, "Intimacy figures centrally in narratives of a life lived right. . . . One of the responsibilities of a human life lived right is an obligation towards intimacy."[21] For example, writing about the presumably single men who frequented the Times Square porn theaters in the 1970s and 80s, Samuel Delany argues, "A glib wisdom holds that people like this just don't want relationships. They have 'problems with intimacy.' But the salient fact is: These *were* relationships. . . . Intimacy for most of us is a condition that endures, however often repeated, for minutes or for hours. And these all had their many intimate hours."[22] I find it difficult to trust Delany here, not because he's wrong, but because the stakes for claiming intimacy are so high. Despite the many queer texts that lean on the concept of intimacy in various ways, these stakes effectively spoil the concept for me as a metric for sex.[23] I can't ignore these stakes or pretend they don't matter.

At the same time, I get Delany's point. At the infamously libertine Berlin club Berghain, I met a middle-aged German woman who I talked to for hours, on and off. She confessed to me that she has three or four kids at home and a square office job, that her coworkers would be shocked to learn that she's a regular at Berghain. Our conversation felt intimate to me, but not only because of this confession; it was the way she'd approached me, asking (in German, at first) if I could distract her from a distressing phone call she'd just received, and in the way she quickly felt like a friend without the history, knowledge, or experience that friends typically share. We immediately enjoyed each other's company, or so it seemed to me. She was personable and charming, and it didn't hurt that I was on MDMA. I later spotted her across the dance floor getting ready to leave. I shouted her name. She looked around but couldn't locate me; the music was too loud. This happened two more times and then she was gone.

Contra Delany, one might respond to the valuing of intimacy by valuing impersonality instead; by identifying some social, political, or psychological utility to keeping people at a distance, allowing them to stay mysterious and enigmatic. This is the approach Leo Bersani takes in "Is the Rectum a Grave?" Cruising is valuable, Bersani argues, precisely because it is impersonal. Prototypically, there is no first date in cruising, no dressing up (especially when you start out naked), no polite conversation, no best foot forward, no witty banter, no backstory, no innuendo, no nightcap, no second date, no first sleepover, no getting to know each other, no lowering your guard, no meeting the family. There may be seduction—posing, glancing, playing hard to get—but the aim is impersonality.

It is not only impersonality that matters to Bersani, but more precisely impersonality in the context of sex. In contemporary American culture, sex is typically thought to be intimate—even when anonymous—not only because we are physically close and vulnerable during sex, but because nakedness, arousal, and penetration are socially constructed as dirty (hence the requirement of privacy); participating in this dirtiness can make us emotionally, interpersonally, and socially vulnerable as well. Bersani coins the apparently paradoxical phrase "impersonal intimacy" to characterize the kind of interpersonal relation that cruising tends to produce: physically intimate yet socially/psychologically impersonal. Bersani modifies the noun "intimacy" with the adjective "impersonal" to suggest that these relational modes can coexist and that they might produce something new when they do.

Bersani's interest in impersonal intimacy stems from a psychoanalytic understanding of the ego as characteristically paranoid and aggressive in its mission to safeguard our sense of self.[24] Because of our self-protective egos, we worry that strangers might possess some kind of significant and threatening difference from us.[25] In an effort to quell this anxiety, we try to gather knowledge about other people and to sort them into categories: same as us or different from us, in part according to social criteria: gender, sexuality, race, class, and so on.[26] For the ego, same is safe, and different is dangerous. While social difference represents a psychic threat to the self, at least its contours appear to be knowable, unlike mysterious, enigmatic otherness.[27]

Designations of same and different shape our interpersonal relations, but also social relations more broadly. If others are determined to be different from us, then to stay safe we might need to erect physical barriers like gated communities, border walls, prisons, and camps to contain or keep them out, or else to convert them; this conclusion is more characteristic of the right. On the other hand, if others are determined to be the same as us then they can be allowed in and assimilated; this conclusion is more typical of the left. For the left in the US, what appears to be difference is often revealed to be sameness—love is love, undocumented migrants work just as hard as citizens do (or harder!), Black people care about their families just like white people do, and so on. In this way, the ethical left can be as uncomfortable with otherness, as intolerant of difference as the defensive right, though this discomfort and intolerance assume a different form: assimilation rather than expulsion or conversion.

Of course, difference can also be a turn-on, sexually speaking. In fact, -philic and phobic responses to difference can be related, as Frantz Fanon theorizes.[28] For example, while a "fetish" for raced or classed others might seem to indicate a nonviolent or even hospitable orientation toward raced or classed difference, motivated by a desire to commune with difference rather than eliminate it, psychoanalysis proposes that fetishes are still fundamentally self-protective, an idea I explore in more detail in the next chapter.

This psychoanalytic explanation of intolerance might seem profoundly anti-sociological. Where psychoanalysis universalizes—we all have an ego that operates similarly—sociology particularizes: the desire to demystify other people might be differently explained depending on one's social location.[29] A sociologically minded person might read the psychoanalytic explanation above and think, "Maybe that's why wealthy, white, hetero,

Judeo-Christian, cis men from the global North want to know about other people." (Fanon: "In the French Antilles 97 percent of the families cannot produce one Oedipal neurosis.")[30] As the old joke goes: What do you mean "we," white man? Then again, sociology as a discipline might be understood as an expression of the ego's compulsion to resolve mysterious otherness into knowable sameness and difference; shall we find out whether social others' desires, perspectives, values, and experiences are the same as ours or not? If situating knowledge production "within particular intellectual, historical, and political contexts and moments (and not others)" offers an alternative to universalizing theories that incorporate but disavow authors' (typically privileged) social positions, as Margot Weiss argues, this knowledge may nevertheless be desired by others—that is, readers—because it allows the ego to relax, not unlike ethnography in the bad old days.[31] The question remains: Who wants to know, and why?

Somewhat paradoxically, the universalizing nature of psychoanalysis makes it susceptible to the same critique. In other words, the idea of a universally defensive ego might be appealing insofar as it means that there is no significant difference between us and others; we're all basically the same. The paradox (or aporia) is that this accusation only makes sense within the psychoanalytic framework that it undermines.

What redeems psychoanalysis from this sociological critique, in my view, is its speculative approach to understanding.[32] At its best, psychoanalysis doesn't aim to produce objective, unassailable truths, but rather interpretations. For me, engaging psychoanalysis—especially within an autotheoretical framework—is a way of answering Kane Race's call for scholars to bring "speculation, play and experimentation" into our work.[33] For this reason, I was surprised by Joan Acocella's assertion, in a review of psychoanalyst Adam Phillips's oeuvre, that "part of what makes psychoanalytic writing such a chore to get through is its dogmatism, its laying down of the law—and about matters for which there is no support from evidence, let alone from common sense."[34] (For the record, Acocella does not find Phillips dogmatic.) Despite its universalizing claims, I appreciate psychoanalysis as an invitation to differ. Psychoanalytic explanations are not true or false, but rather compelling or unpersuasive, raising the question: Why are we drawn to this or that explanation, if not for objective truth? As Phillips writes, "We should not ask . . . is the author right, but is he bitter? And if so, what about exactly? Not, what does she believe, but what does she dread?"[35] Psychoanalysis invites us to think about how what we know—or believe we know—is shaped by our own desires: those we're aware of, those we struggle with, and those we can't bear to acknowledge.

❡

For Bersani, the impersonal intimacy of cruising is important because it effectively allows us to relax about strangers' otherness, disarming our anxious egos. He explains:

> In cruising—at least in ideal cruising—we leave our selves behind. The gay bathhouse is especially favorable to ideal cruising because, in addition to the opportunity anonymous sex offers its practitioners of shedding much of the personality that individuates them psychologically, the common bathhouse uniform—a towel—communicates very little (although there are of course ways of wearing a towel . . .) about our social personality (economic privilege, class status, taste, and so on). Most important, the intimacy of bodies no longer embellished or impoverished, protected or exposed, by the "clothing" of both dress and character offers an exceptional experience of the infinite distance that separates us from all otherness.[36]

Here Bersani observes that our individual and social "personalities"—typically expressed through the " 'clothing' of both dress and character"—are muted in the bathhouse. The word "clothing" alludes to the multiple means through which we perform our selves for others, including actual clothing, but also ostensibly things like conversation. With our personalities muted, it becomes easier to apprehend and accept the fundamental unknowability of other people, and maybe of ourselves, not simply because we have become impersonal to each other, but because we've been "intimate" while maintaining impersonality. The fact that we can take pleasure in estrangement is thus key to Bersani's interest in cruising, and to his proposition that it enacts a less violent way of being with others.

Even more than the bathhouse, I think the glory hole exemplifies Bersani's notion of impersonal intimacy. If our personalities are muted in the bathhouse, they are silenced in the glory hole, because both partners' faces and bodies are mostly obscured. As Dave Holmes, Patrick O'Byrne, and Stuart J. Murray observe, the glory hole "affords an intense, temporary escape from the demands of subjectivity" and, relatedly, intersubjectivity.[37]

They elaborate: "The hole and the wall break the circuit of mirrored reciprocity; not only is the user not face-to-face with the other, he is not face-to-face with himself, that is, he is not forced to face the other as a reflection of himself, as an embodiment of his own desire, which may be shameful or otherwise intolerable to him."[38] This leads Holmes, O'Byrne, and Murray to conclude that glory hole sex "is not sex with a 'whole person,' but what is?"[39] This might be why casual, anonymous sex is sometimes pathologized: not because it is fundamentally superficial, but because it suggests that there might not be a knowable subject hiding beneath the surface, waiting to be uncovered, rescued, cared for, or loved, just roles and scripts that we're attached to and invited to follow. Only surface, no depth.[40] I explore this idea in more detail in the next chapter.

One of the challenges of teaching Bersani to undergrads is that many of them find it hard to believe that anyone would celebrate sex that involves moving "irresponsibly among other bodies, somewhat indifferent to them."[41] What about altruism, kindness, care, and love? When Bersani characterizes impersonal intimacy as a "superficial view of human relations" and talks about treating other people as "[opportunities], at once insignificant and precious, for narcissistic pleasures," students assume that he must be opposed to these things.[42] Who would argue in favor of irresponsibility, indifference, superficiality, and narcissism? It helps to remind them that Bersani believes that thwarting processes of identification/differentiation can subvert the motive for intersubjective violence. The idea here is that would-be homophobes, for example, might relax if only their egos were less preoccupied with identifying with or differentiating from other people according to gender/sexual desire and behavior. This might sound utopian, but it's precisely what Bersani is suggesting could happen through sex. I'm amused by the notion that homophobic men don't need to be convinced that gay people are harmless, but rather should be experimenting with buttplay, not to "turn them" gay exactly, but rather to open them up to the pleasures of self-shattering.[43] At the same time, I'm rather attached to my objects of desire, with all their alluring, presumed difference. Must I really give up my "fetishes" for the cause?

Bersani is hardly alone in critiquing identity. When the term "queer" was reclaimed, it was precisely in opposition to gender and sexual identification as a technique of social control. As Steven Seidman explains:

> Queers did not claim to represent a new identity but a "position" of criticism toward the idea that gender and sexuality can or should be thought of as consisting of a set of fixed roles and identities, some of which are normal and others of which are deviant. . . . To be queer represents a desire to be freed of the thick social regulations centered on gender and sexual identities, especially in a social order that enforces the normative status of heterosexuality and mutually exclusive, antithetical gender identities.[44]

At Wesleyan and other progressive institutions in the US, people often use the term "queer" as a catch-all for non-hetero sexualities, as "BIPOC" is used to group together all non-white racial identities. But I prefer the idea that queerness stands outside of identity, in opposition to it—for the reasons that Seidman, Michael Warner, and other queer thinkers have elaborated. This is not just about queerness, but about all sexuality. As Dean puts it succinctly, "Sex is not the expression of identity but its undoing. Identity politics is no friend of psychoanalysis."[45]

In queer thought, the refusal or disinclination to identify sexually is sometimes valued as a means to a kind of universalism. It's not that we're all the same in the absence of identity categories that tell us who we're like and not like. Rather, we're better able to see others as particular, or as similarly different. To take one example, in an article titled "All Sound Is Queer," Drew Daniel celebrates how noisy the world can be, and how—because it is difficult to close our ears—the intrusion of sound from the outside world "affords us the possibility of forgetting our 'me-ist' attachments to our subjective particularity and affiliation."[46] Daniel suggests that our subjectivity is undone (if only partially and temporarily) when we have no choice but to hear the world: birds, traffic, car stereos, other people's conversations, and so on. This is why we sometimes experience these sounds as annoying; it can be unpleasant to lose a sense of oneself. At the same time, Daniel is hopeful that the experience of being undone "might also constitute our human community as precisely the queer indifference of having nothing in common." Tom Roach usefully theorizes this indifference as a kind of fungibility, drawing from Bersani, Foucault, and Guy Hocquenghem.[47]

Daniel asks a similar question as Bersani here: What might a community without identification or differentiation look like? Could you even call it a community if the only thing we share is that we are all alone in our particularity, all susceptible to the intrusion of the world outside ourselves? As Bersani muses, "What is different about others (their psychological individuality) could be thought of as merely the envelope of the more profound (if less fully realized, or completed) part of themselves which is our sameness. . . . The experience of belonging to a family of singularity without national, ethnic, racial, or gendered borders might make us sensitive to the ontological status of difference itself as . . . the nonthreatening supplement of sameness."[48] Again, Bersani is suggesting here that subverting the need to identify with and differentiate from other people might allow us to relax about their otherness because we'd all essentially be in the same boat—no one inherently safer or more threatening than anyone else. We would all be strange, even to ourselves. He describes this as feeling at home in the world rather than antagonized by it.[49]

This queer universalism (to use Madhavi Menon's term) might be appealing to some on the left when framed in opposition to "dominant neoliberal capitalist democratic culture" (Daniel's words).[50] It becomes less appealing when framed as an expression of a white, cis male desire to avoid dealing with race or gender, as in José Esteban Muñoz's characterization of "antirelational queer theories"—associated with Bersani and Lee Edelman, though neither adopts the label—as "wishful thinking, investments in deferring various dreams of difference," and then, more succinctly and fatally, as "the gay white man's last stand."[51] Muñoz is essentially proposing that queer universalism is really just white, cis male universalism in disguise, an iteration of the white desire for colorblindness and an expression of white privilege.[52]

Muñoz could be read as making a strategic argument for maintaining identity categories; maybe we'd be better off without them, but we need to preserve them to combat identity-based oppression. Acting as if identities don't exist or are counterproductive makes it difficult or impossible to do this. As long as there is anti-Black racism in the US, we need "Black." As long as there is misogyny, misogynoir, and transmisogynoir, we need "woman." As Cathy J. Cohen writes, "Because of my multiple identities, which locate me and other 'queer' people of color at the margins in this country, my material advancement, my physical protection and my emotional well-being are constantly threatened. In those stable categories and named communities whose histories have been structured by shared resistance to oppression, I find relative degrees of safety and security."[53]

One might make a similar argument for the category "gay": as long as there is homophobia, we need "gay." My disinclination or refusal to identify as gay would not stop a group of drunk bros from cornering me outside a bathhouse and telling me a homophobic joke. (This happened to me in Berlin.) Despite my refusal to identify as gay, homophobes nonetheless have some idea—or fantasy—of what I've been doing in there and will assign me an identity whether I want it or not. More to the point, without a group identifier like "gay," how can you stop homophobic violence, let alone comprehend it?[54] As E. Patrick Johnson asks, "What is the utility of queer theory on the front lines, in the trenches, on the street, or anyplace where the racialized and sexualized body is beaten, starved, fired, cursed—indeed, where the body is the site of trauma?"[55]

I have reservations about Muñoz's critique of queer universalism. One of the purposes of queer universalism, as I understand it, is to become more uncertain about the stability and coherence of identity categories, rather than simply wishing them away or pretending they don't exist; less "I don't see race," for example, than "I'm not certain what I'm seeing when I see race."[56] For Edelman, often accused of ignoring race, queerness is like Blackness or femaleness in terms of what he calls "ontological negation," though queerness may be particularly well positioned to resist the impulse to "return to a substantive identity" (that is, a queer person) or, in Lacanian terms, to avoid confusing the "contingency of the social" with the "structural law of the Symbolic" because of the long-standing theorization of queerness as outside (and in opposition to) identity.[57] Like Muñoz, I may be guilty of this confusion, if that's what it is, with my interest in "'constructed' sociological entities," though, unlike Muñoz, I find appealing the idea of undoing these entities.[58]

I also suspect that Muñoz's critique of the antisocial thesis sublimates a desire to police the passive, flighty, irresponsible queers who are unwilling or unable to become proper political subjects capable of organized resistance, whether or not they are gay white men; in my experience, moralizers on the left rarely embrace or even acknowledge their ambition for power.[59] That said, if queer universalism does appeal more to gay white men than to BIPOC non-hetero people, this might not simply express gay white men's avoidance of race- and gender-based oppression; it might also have something to do with the ways that forms of oppression vary from each other.

Because sexuality concerns our desires and pleasures, it remains a mystery until declared, though gender non-normativity may mark you as suspicious, as it did for me in childhood, and though we may be attributed a sexual identity by others if we're "caught in the act." Even when self-declared, sexual identification expresses an untenable certainty about our own desire and what might bring us pleasure, as Dean and Oliver Davis argue.[60] Like sexuality, race is a social construct subject to transformation, but it is generally neither a mystery nor a product of self-evaluation, even as racial self-identification can differ from racial attribution. As Wesley Morris observes of Blackness, "In the United States, a Black self eventually discovers his race is a form of credit (or discredit, as it were). You can't leave home without it."[61] Because sexuality in the contemporary US is constructed primarily around desire and pleasure, a person who is assumed to be straight—typically in relation to their normative gender expression—but who identifies as gay has been misunderstood. Because race is constructed primarily around phenotype, which is to say legible bodily characteristics like skin color, a person who is seen as white but identifies as Black is not typically considered to be misunderstood, but rather foolish, or—like Rachel Dolezal—a fraud, especially without a Black biological parent or grandparent. A person who is seen as Black but does not identify as Black is also not typically considered to be misunderstood, but—like OJ Simpson or Tiger Woods—naive, delusional, or self-hating.

To a certain extent, sexual desire isn't completely illegible; it can be hazily legible, imperfectly refracted through racialized gender. The childhood bullies who called me *faggot* were right about my desire, generally speaking, but they were making an educated guess based on my femininity in relation to my social position as viewed from their own. We can transform some of our gendered traits—within limits determined, in part, by our racialization and bodily characteristics like height and frame—altering the way our sexuality is perceived by others, whether we intend to or not. The longer and more unkempt my beard, the deeper my voice, and the frumpier my clothes, the more that strangers assume I'm straight. But no matter how I modify my appearance, I will always be seen and treated as white in the US and, therefore, will always be white for all intents and purposes. I suspect that the same (or similar) is true for gay BIPOC men, though the gendered traits in question and the ways in which they are modified may vary, and the performance of gender/sexuality may be impelled in particular ways in relation to racism.

It's possible that my interest in dismantling identity has something to do with the way that homophobia monopolizes my experience of being oppressed, and sexuality is largely an internal affair, if no less relational or context dependent than race, for example. In heteronormative environments, I often feel very gay. But in some gay bars and clubs, including those patronized mostly by white, non-trans men, I feel very queer. And in some queer spaces, I feel oddly gay again, but in a different way. When I travel abroad, "gay" (or its linguistic translation) may have different meanings that are more or less desirable to me, depending on the other categories on offer. Maybe queer universalism appeals to me, in part, because I feel more comfortable in and receptive to the world outside myself when categorical inclusion and exclusion are less of a thing, and I'm reluctant—in this context—to make a virtue of feeling uncomfortable or to otherwise critique my desire for comfort, for example, as an expression of my privilege.

When sexual non-normativity comes up in Intro to Sociology, I often make a point of telling students that I love being a gay man. I actually feel ambivalent about the identity—and about identifying sexually at all, given that it's my decision—but I want them to know that I resent the notion (implicit in "born this way" rhetoric) that nobody would choose to be gay.[62] I was surprised and a little heartbroken when a queer student once earnestly asked me if I could be more specific about what I love, as if he couldn't fathom the notion. It's a big gay world, but I ad-libbed a list: the humor; the moxie and resilience; the flamboyance and fanfare; the sensitivity, melancholy, and bookishness; the sexual licentiousness; the interest in domesticity and material things (especially architecture, interiors, and design); the esoteric curiosities and fandoms; the eccentric characters; some of the music, television, film, and art; and the independence and creativity of building a life outside the strictures of heteronorms.

Because non-hetero people are everywhere, our culture is heterogeneous to the point of fracture; it makes more sense to talk about non-hetero cultures—plural—given the ways that our multiple identities shape the desires and pleasures identified as sexual, the names we give to the groups both big and small that seem to share our desires and pleasures, and the variety of cultural forms these groups develop. Despite this heterogeneity, non-hetero cultures share something important: they are generally not a family affair, passed down from parents to children, though some of us may learn from our non-hetero "elders" and the cultural ether.[63] Like many gay men of my era in the US, I was ushered into gayness alone, and I learned to deal with its non-normativity privately—and virtually, as Chris Stedman writes—particularly in the absence of support from my peers, school, healthcare providers, and government.[64] My family was accepting and would have been supportive had I not been mortified by the prospect of discussing anything remotely related to sex with them. Before I'd heard the term "queer" used in the contemporary sense, I made up a kind of gayness for myself and carried it with me wherever I went, sometimes encountering like-minded weirdos along the way. This might also inform my willingness to leave the identity behind; it never felt all that shared to begin with.

The appeal of queer universalism need not be some kind of transcendental ethic; it could also be about the sex it makes possible. For example, I fantasize that the unraveling of sexual identity might supply me with at least a few masculine, formerly straight guys to fuck, once they're no longer concerned with shoring up their hetero identities and are more willing to "experiment."[65] Some hetero non-trans guys seem to believe that every gay man on earth would fuck them if given half a chance, not because they're necessarily hot, but insofar as they're masculine. Or is it because they know firsthand how indiscriminate male sexuality can be? Maybe that's why some of us make it publicly known that we won't have sex with just any guy; even hetero guys must want to feel chosen sometimes.

There are other reasons that marginalized groups might be attached to their identities. Drawing from Nietzsche, Kathi Weeks asks:

> Can we want, are we willing to create, a new world that would no longer be "our" world, a social form that would not produce subjects like us? . . . What would it mean to respond to the prospect of our own "perishing" in a different future, a future in which neither we nor our children—to note that common trope by which we still might imagine a place for ourselves, or people bearing family resemblances to ourselves—would exist, and to respond, moreover, not with fear and anxiety but with joy and hope?[66]

I don't have children, but I do have queer students who were neither bullied nor closeted. I envy their experience, or what I imagine it to be, though it makes them more difficult for me to relate to, to identify with. Of course I'd rather the world be less homophobic, but I also wonder if this would make me feel existentially lonely because my gender and sexuality were shaped by the homophobic environment in which I grew up. The prospect of feeling existentially lonely doesn't exactly inspire joy or hope in me, though I imagine I'd feel other ways too, like relieved.

Citing Wendy Brown, Weeks also argues that "identity politics fueled by *ressentiment* 'becomes deeply invested in its own impotence, even while it seeks to assuage its pain through its vengeful moralizing, through its wide distribution of suffering, through its reproach to power as such.'"[67] I think I've been guilty of this at times, relying on the type of straight people—white, middle-class, conservative suburbanites—I grew up around as easy targets of derision, especially when they're explicitly homophobic, but also racist, misogynist, classist, xenophobic, or ableist (all of which were common among my peers in New Jersey). Whether or not my anger, melancholy, or *ressentiment* is always justified, I have taken a kind of satisfaction in my contempt for this particular slice of the hetero world. I wonder if I'd still feel angry if (hetero)sexual identity were less of a thing, and what I would do with this anger. Would it fester with no outlet? Would I find an appropriate surrogate, or direct it inward at my own failure to get over it?

☙

When I cruise, do I experience the "infinite distance that separates us from all otherness," as Bersani muses, or do I remain committed to sorting potential partners according to their measurable distance from the identities I occupy? Has cruising induced in me a feeling of being at home in the world, of being unperturbed by other people's potentially threatening difference from me? Has my anxious ego been disarmed by the pleasures of anonymous sex? I'm amused by the idea that such a profound transformation might happen at a rest area, or in a steam room between a handful of horny guys on their way home from work, though I remain uninterested in the redemption it offers.

For any of this to happen, Bersani suggests, our psychological and social personalities need to be muted; otherwise we see only other people's similarities to and differences from us. This might be easier said than done; there is a lot of meaning attached to our bodily matter. I'm often struck by the variety of men who patronize the spa, by their different bodies—tall and short; fat, thin, and muscular; young and old; white, brown, Black, and Asian; smooth and hairy; cocks of every shape and size. It sometimes feels like the setup for a joke, or like a pornographic Benetton ad.

To state the obvious, few of these characteristics are without sociological meaning; bodily matter is raced, classed, gendered, nationalized, able-bodied or disabled. Sexual attraction is never just about looks; it's also about the social meanings attached to our bodies. These meanings can ignite or extinguish our lust. For example, a guy cruising the spa isn't simply more hirsute or stocky—to me he's more masculine, particularly if these characteristics aren't accompanied by legibly feminine qualities. This is why many of us modify our bodies—shaping and adorning them through diet, exercise, and supplements; tanning and bleaching; tattoos and piercings; cutting, dying, and styling hair; grooming body and facial hair; cosmetics, lotions, cleansers, toners, and ointments; spa treatments and plastic surgery—we are trying to make our bodies mean in different ways. It would be physically uncomfortable and socially awkward to wear a flannel shirt or basketball shorts in a steam room, but you can try to walk, sit, and scowl like a man. The meanings that inform our desires are not abandoned at the bathhouse door. If anything, they become more prominent in an environment that limits exposure to contradictory information: "the 'clothing' of both dress and character."[68] It's an unfortunate state of affairs when you don't like the meanings attached to your bodily matter, and when this matter is difficult or impossible to change. I tend to look my age when I'm naked, and to other guys that increasingly means "daddy," whether I like it or not.

These meanings—and the words used to describe them—are the building blocks of desire. A body with a certain quantity and density of hair in particular places becomes "furry"—a hotter word than "hairy," in my opinion. A furry body that is fat in particular ways and lacks the markers of youth becomes a "bear." Language organizes the infinite variability of appearance, desire, and behavior into types and other categories: twink, jock, bear, otter, hung, cut/uncut, smooth/hairy, top/bottom/vers, masculine/feminine. As Dean notes, these terms have a tendency to proliferate, especially in gay culture.[69] "Bear" has yielded "cub" (young bear), "polar bear" (old bear), and "muscle bear." Using these terms has as much to do with our fantasies and desires as it does with empirical description, as anyone who enjoys talking dirty during sex intuitively understands. Every time someone on Grindr asks me if I'm gay, bi, or straight, I think less about the contours of my desire than I do about the term(s) they're hoping I'll claim and why.

Bersani is clearly aware of this. In "Is the Rectum a Grave?" he describes the bathhouse as a scene of harsh evaluation:

> Anyone who has ever spent one night in a gay bathhouse knows that it is (or was) one of the most ruthlessly ranked,

hierarchized, and competitive environments imaginable. Your looks, muscles, hair distribution, size of cock, and shape of ass determined exactly how happy you were going to be during those few hours, and rejection, generally accompanied by two or three words at most, could be swift and brutal, with none of the civilizing hypocrisies with which we get rid of undesirables in the outside world.[70]

I've witnessed such brutal rejection many times at the spa. On one occasion, I was sitting next to a guy in the hot tub—young, white, chubby, short, and smooth, with a smaller-than-average dick—when a much older white guy came in and sat down across from us. The younger guy turned to me, grimaced and whispered, "Gross," and then got up and left. While I was not surprised by his harsh judgment, I didn't expect him to verbalize it; he was hardly conventionally attractive himself. Furthermore, the older guy hadn't initiated contact with either of us. His very presence was enough to offend the younger guy.

I'd like to read Bersani as suggesting not that cruisers don't see identity and difference, or that markers of identity and difference become meaningless in cruising, but rather that these markers stop functioning as indicators of some kind of internal state, essence, or truth. The less we know about our partners—their feelings, perceptions, self-image, past experiences, and so on—the more we can imagine them as we want, or not imagine them at all, depending on the material they give us to work with. In the largest hot tub at the spa, material is often scant—just the sensation of legs brushing underwater, or the odd weightlessness of a flaccid penis—which underscores to me just how much sex with other people can be a solo affair.[71]

If I do experience my partner's otherness, or rather my distance from all otherness, it's not because I'm ignoring his girthy dick, furry chest, or stoic face, or because I'm failing to read his masculinity. It's because the impersonality of our sex has sensitized me to the fact that this has little to do with him as a person. Who knows (or cares) about his biography? Who knows (or cares) what might be going on for him: who he wants to be or believes himself to be, what he desires from me, what turns him on about me or our interaction? It's like the closer I get to a stranger physically, the more acutely estranged I feel from him in every other way.

In this sense, Bersani seems to underestimate how differentiating ourselves from strangers can entice us to engage with and take pleasure in otherness, especially if we suspect that some mysterious otherness lurks behind knowable difference.[72] My knowledge of masculine, working-class men is sketchy, which makes them good fodder for my fantasies, and hopefully vice versa. At the same time, the impersonality of our sex prevents it from becoming a reconnaissance mission.

This is not to say that we ought to engage with or take pleasure in otherness for ethical reasons. For one, ethics itself can ironically be a form of subjugating those identified as unethical—whether through shaming, intimidating, or reserving affirmation and affection for those deemed good—especially when ethics requires others to think and act like oneself. As Phillips reminds us, morality is inconceivable without intimidation, though it may be justified by "protectiveness, chosenness, destiny, love."[73] I'm not trying to accuse those with ethical commitments of being hypocritically unethical. Rather, I'm proposing that we all deal with our aggression in different ways, including by sublimating it into ethics or, as Bersani argues, love.[74] In fact, there may be no sexuality without the aggression of the ego, persistently sending out its echolocation signals to determine whether others are a threat to the self. This effort seems designed to see oneself reflected back—no threatening difference found; system reset—except for the uneasy pleasure of not being able to tell.

Phillips's argument is not so ethically motivated. He seems more concerned with the pleasures and terrors of giving up control than with protecting the objects of our control. Like Bersani, he may be interested in the promise of a less violent world, but he shifts focus from the targets of aggression to the agents of aggression, from ethics to desire and pleasure. It should be clear by now that one need not be ethically motivated to leave other people alone. As I've suggested, there can be pleasure in maintaining distance from our objects of desire, in not knowing them. For many cruisers, this is the point of cruising. When I have sex with a stranger in a steam room, I'm not trying to protect him by not asking invasive questions, or inquiring about his feelings, or trying to figure out his deal; I'm safeguarding my own pleasure.

Maybe some cruisers are ethical exemplars, even when motivated primarily by lust. If the sex I desire happens to offer some greater utility that interests me, I'm not going to refuse it or refuse to acknowledge it. But it's a little disingenuous and self-aggrandizing to celebrate this utility as if it were the point. Nonviolence is never the point for me, and it shouldn't have to be. The point of cruising at the spa is pleasure, and I may find it in a kind of distance from otherness, but I also find it elsewhere: in the aggression of making a move without knowing how it will be received; in the ego flattery of being pursued by someone desirable; in the overwhelming and disorienting sensation of being touched underwater by several pairs of hands I can't see; in finally hooking up with a hot guy after a tantalizing period of observing, waiting, anticipating, and strategizing;[75] in the unspoiled fantasy of a macho, macho man; in the frisson of prohibited contact undetected by non-cruising patrons; in the surprise and unpredictability of being cruised by and having sex with a Hasidic Jew for the first time; in the euphoric facial expression of a guy who sat below me on the floor of the steam room and took my foot into his mouth while he masturbated; and in the excessive, unbridled horniness of a group of men jerking each other off under the ever-present threat of interruption.

Can desirable politics be found in these assorted pleasures? Do they serve a therapeutic function, perhaps compensating me for the shame of the various stigmas with which I've been saddled? Or maybe the opposite is the case: The pleasures are politically problematic and psychically damaging. While not uninteresting, these questions ask too much of sex. As generative as I find Bersani's argument, its vision of sex is constrained by its political imperative, reducing the manifold pleasures of cruising to an engagement with otherness. This political imperative captures my imagination as much as it places a limit on where it can go. Given my political upbringing, my interest in the world often depends on finding its politics, but I'd like to believe that a political imagination need not become a political imperative, and inquisitiveness need not become an inquisition.

3

Labels Are for People

Grindr's primary interface is a grid of images, displayed in order of geographic proximity.[1] In most of the places I've lived and traveled, the grid is dominated by photographs of faces and naked torsos. Tapping on any user's photo takes you to his profile, which typically contains descriptive information like age, height, weight, and sexual interests. But it's not uncommon for users to send messages without first looking at each other's profiles; as with many hookup and dating apps, image is everything.[2]

Like many guys on Grindr, I engineer my profile to attract hot guys by making the most of what I've got while also attending to the fact that whatever I post is public and therefore visible to other people: students, friends, co-workers, exes.[3] Because I'm generally not attracted to my own type—that is, guys whose bodies and faces resemble mine—evaluating my attractiveness is an intellectual exercise; it's something I have to think about, because I don't feel it. This may be my most heterosexual quality, with an unfortunate queer twist: unlike straight people, I could potentially be my own type, but I'm not, so it's hard to find myself attractive, despite whatever success I've had attracting my objects of desire.

To make myself feel more attractive, I play with and modify my appearance in ways that make me look more like the guys I find hot, though there are some things that just can't be changed. I also pay attention to the ways that guys respond to me: What is it about me that they seem to like, if anything? Some of them share my taste, at least in part. They say they like my beard, and I respond that I like theirs. I feel flattered by the compliment and also gratified; it's not just that I can grow a beard, but that I choose to grow it, and I groom it well. I feel less flattered when guys are turned on by things that I have no control over, even when our desires align.

Some of my objects of desire don't share my taste. In fact, some of them are turned on by the very things I am most insecure about, like my thinning, graying hair. When this happens, I have to negotiate between what I need to feel attractive and what they find hot. I'm not going to stop taking Minoxidil, but neither will I swat their hand away from my repulsive scalp, even though drawing attention to it makes me feel unsexy. And sometimes they are turned on by qualities that I too find hot, but that I don't recognize as belonging to me. In the middle of sex, a guy once said, "I love your tight, furry body." *That's not how I would describe it,* I thought, *but I'll go with it.* He was the furry one, truly covered in hair, beefy with broad shoulders and strong arms, and a deep, hoarse voice that made me sound like Mickey Mouse in comparison. If I looked and sounded like him, I would feel so undeniably hot, but whatever: If he wants to fuck someone with a "tight, furry body," then I'm going to try my best to embody that body. This is also to say that when I modify my appearance, I consider why I'm desired and what role or position I will be expected to occupy based on the way I look and present myself.

For me, Grindr pics serve two primary functions. The first is obvious: to give people a sense of what you will look like in person and how you will act. When someone doesn't look like their pics, we might accuse them of misrepresenting themselves or, worse, of lying. For example, like many men who are insecure about balding, I think I look better in a hat; let's call it lying by omission. When I post or send a pic of myself in a hat, some guys undoubtedly imagine a full head of thick, dark hair under there. A friend of mine once went home with a guy who excused himself to the bathroom to remove his toupee. "If he's wearing a hat in every pic," another friend tells me, "he's definitely bald." My ego can't handle the look of disappointment on a guy's face when he realizes he's been sold a bill of goods, so my profile includes at least one photo sans hat.

I'm not turned off by baldness; I find some guys attractive—even more attractive—with a smooth scalp, but the head has to be right, and it has to be on the right body. Neither my head nor my body is right. Or maybe the problem isn't my head or body, but rather my self-image. When I was younger, I was desired for being cute—like many young, white, skinny boys. While I found this somewhat infantilizing, I also came to understand it as my capital in the dating/hookup market, though it contradicted my own desire for older, tougher, and more rugged men.

I don't mind attracting guys in ways that contradict my own desire and self-image, though I might feel different if I were differently embodied.

These days, "cutie" has been replaced by "daddy." I don't think of myself as a daddy yet, but neither do I take offense; it's an invitation, an opportunity. Nobody starts out as a daddy. All daddies used to be something else. Many used to be twinks. Maybe I'll enjoy the role at some point. Maybe the idea of inhabiting authority will become erotic to me, and when I inspect my receding hair line in the mirror, I will read it as a manifestation of my authority and be pleased by its hotness, the way that guys who call me "daddy" seem to be.

The second and less obvious function of Grindr pics is related to this role play: Like mirrors, photographs are useful in experimenting with altering how we appear and what our appearance might mean. This isn't a question of representing or misrepresenting ourselves, but of using images to change ourselves. It can be transformative to see a picture of yourself in which you look more feminine, masculine, pretty, handsome, delicate, strong, confident, outdoorsy, artsy, carefree, or whatever quality you might desire. *Is that really me?* Seeing might not be believing, but it can help. Posting these pics in your profile can also help, if strangers agree to see you in this new way and treat you as such. As I experimented with appearing more masculine in my Grindr pics, I was increasingly solicited by guys who'd write "hey man" or "what's up buddy." This felt awkward at first, but with repetition it felt more familiar and comfortable.

This isn't unique to Grindr. Many of us are reasonably proficient at sculpting ourselves in various ways to elicit desired responses from others "in real life." Some of us then use these responses to prove to ourselves that we are, in fact, whoever we are seen to be. It's an impressive psychic sleight of hand: working so hard at something only to conclude later that it comes naturally. But Grindr does make it easier for users to craft impressions than it may be when we're face-to-face with someone because it gives us time to choose our words and photos carefully. For example, it's more difficult to change your voice and how you speak in person than it is to channel a new voice in text. For this reason, interactions on Grindr can feel particularly calculated, but also more open to relational and erotic experimentation, a process Kane Race terms "sexual speculation."[4]

It doesn't always work out. As Jean-Paul Sartre famously writes in *No Exit*, "Hell is other people." In his commentary for a 1965 recording of the play, Sartre clarifies the line: "If our relations with others are twisted or corrupted, then others have to be hell. . . . Fundamentally, others are what is most important in us for understanding ourselves."[5] Sartre is suggesting that since we understand ourselves primarily through the eyes of others, it can be destabilizing and destructive when something in a relationship isn't working the way we want it to. We need other people in order to form ourselves, but it's a risky, uncertain endeavor; what they see in us—and want from us—might not align with who we believe we are, or who we want to be. As Adam Phillips writes:

> Being misrepresented is simply being presented a version of ourselves—an invention—that we cannot agree with. But we are daunted by other people making us up, by the number of people we seem to be. We become frantic trying to keep the numbers down, trying to keep the true story of who we really are in circulation. This, perhaps more than anything else, drives us into the arms of one special partner. Monogamy is a way of getting the versions of ourselves down to a minimum. And, of course, a way of convincing ourselves that some versions are truer than others—that some *are* special.[6]

If monogamy allows us to ignore the other selves we might be, Grindr allows us to experiment with these selves, especially when there's a lot of turnover; more users can mean more opportunities for rapid self-transformation, depending on what you're working with and where you're working with it. I've been "daddy" one minute and "son" the next. If I don't want to occupy either of these roles, I simply don't respond.

I keep this in mind when I look at guys' pics. I try to evaluate their attractiveness, assuming they've been similarly strategic and creative in selecting their pics. I also try to decipher other photographic clues—where they are, what they're wearing, who they're with, their facial expression, the composition of the picture—anything that might indicate what they'll be like in person. I believe that I can learn a lot from the pictures people post: what they look like, how they feel about how they look, how they want to look, and how they want to be seen. There are photographic norms, and I also believe that I can learn something about a person from how they observe or violate these. Or rather, this information allows me to begin to assemble a story in my head about how they might seem in person.

This isn't only about trying to ferret out undesirable qualities that people might try to mute or hide, but also the qualities that they find undesirable and I find desirable. I like a big belly, but some guys will try to minimize their gut in photographs. My investigation continues with the short answer portion of the profile: What do they say, how do they say it, and why? What do they leave out? I continue to assemble a story about them, and attraction blooms or it doesn't.

I try to keep my own profile brief: just a few sentences to suggest that I'm relatively easy going, and not arrogant, sour, or an asshole. I used to shave a few years off my age. Then I turned forty-two and I figured that anyone who would fuck a forty-year-old would probably fuck a forty-two-year-old. I mention my job because I want people to know that I'm nerd-adjacent, and some guys are into that. I can imagine the appeal; I was a fairly deferential student myself. The professor role doesn't turn me on—it's hard to find one's own job hot—but neither does it bother me when guys are into it.

When there is mutual interest on Grindr, a boilerplate conversation often ensues:

hey

hi

what's up

looking, into?

There is something reassuring about patterned conversation, though the routine of it can get tedious. Sometimes I'll try to force a less formulaic conversation that doesn't simply verify that we're both able to fill in the appropriate sections of a predetermined script: top, bottom, vers, or side, host or travel. Many of my queer friends streamline this process. They like someone's pics, ask if they're looking to have sex imminently, verify mutual attraction and compatibility, and five minutes later they're on a bicycle or in an Uber. Whether because of my anxiety, or because I like to suffer a little anticipation, it usually takes me longer than this.

If all goes well, someone eventually shows up at someone else's door (or car door, or wherever), and an image comes to life. I'm often startled by this transformation; even when someone closely resembles their pictures, a moving, three-dimensional person gives off a lot more information than a still, two-dimensional image. And when people don't look like their pictures, it's often because I'd imagined their movements, expression, or voice differently. In other words, they do resemble their pictures, but they don't embody my fantasies.

When an image of someone speaks to my fantasy more than their actual person does, the image can seem oddly truer to me. In other words, rather than judging the misleading image against the real person, I find myself judging the misleading person against the real image and thinking about that image while the person is sitting in front of me. And sometimes a person might not be what I'd imagined, but they still might be desirable in an unanticipated way.

Strangers sometimes seem so familiar to me, it's as if we've met a hundred times before. There's scarcely anything they can say or do to disabuse me of this feeling; they'd only be acting out of character. And sometimes they seem so original that I could never have imagined them, no matter how many images they'd sent, or how long and involved our conversation prior to meeting in person.

No matter how explicitly we've planned the encounter—sharing nudes, specifying roles, detailing desires and fantasies—there are always small, meaningful details that elude communication: the way he kisses, the feel of his skin, his smell and touch, the expression on his face, the things he says or doesn't say, the sounds he makes or doesn't make, his responsiveness or resolve—which I try to read as clues that might tell me something about his desire, his pleasure, or the way he sees me. This is not about getting to know him, accessing the depth beneath the surface, it's just more information, more meaning attached to bodily matter, more opportunities to be turned on or off. Exactly who or what are we to each other in the process of encountering and reacting to all this specificity: A person? A body? Body parts? An object? An intention? A desire? A mirror? I have felt like all of these things. I have seen others in all of these ways.

One of the appeals of cruising in person is that there tends to be little information, as Bersani recognizes. Less information means less risk of being turned off. This is one incentive to keep quiet. How many fantasies have been shattered by a single spoken word? Seventies gay icon Peter Berlin puts it this way: "If you get close and if one talks, everything can be destroyed. . . . Silence is very exciting."[7] There is a lot of information contained in speech and voice; in what you say, how you say it, and how you sound. An ex-boyfriend liked to draw attention to some of my speech patterns. I try to change the way I speak with non-academics so that I don't come off as pretentious—or should I say "putting on airs"—but my sentences remain stubbornly convoluted, filled with clauses and qualifications. Better just to shut up. There may or may not be an ethical reason to keep quiet—if silence entails relaxing about strangers' otherness—but there is definitely an erotic one.

Complaints about the culture of Grindr and the sex it facilitates being too superficial and objectifying are now well rehearsed to the point of exhaustion. Users stand accused of treating each other like objects, and—as a result—of being fake, false, deceitful, or inauthentic in terms of how they represent themselves. Or maybe it's the platform that's the problem, transforming what could have been a beautiful community into a depressing supermarket where all anyone cares about is pretty packaging.

This critique relies on a framework of surface and depth that is inadequate to the task of describing what happens on Grindr. Image is everything on Grindr, but our images do much more than simply representing or misrepresenting who we are; they facilitate an interactive production of an unstable self that uses materials on hand and can transform in real time. In so doing, they facilitate various kinds of communication that affect the character of our relations with others. As Kane Race elaborates, the images we send each other on Grindr "function as gestural acts that seek to do things beyond the scope of referentiality and representation: they clarify intentions, specify interests, generate particular terms of exchange while setting out the social implications of subsequent connection."[8] Adopting this kind of framework entails moving from "we only care about looks" and "we're not who we appear to be" to "looks are never just a surface but are also a kind of depth" and "depth is not a stable essence but an impression produced through repetition, desire, and conviction."

There is another problem with the complaint that Grindr is objectifying, which contains within in it the command that users treat each other like human beings rather than objects. For many of us, full-resolution humans don't turn us on; other people are an erotic means, not an end. As Phillips argues, "Our lovers are just a prompt or a hint there to remind us of our own erotic delirium, the people who connect us to somewhere else. People, that is to say, who are gods and goddesses in spite of themselves; because as people our lovers are too complicated to excite us. The erotic is a simplification."[9] Our objects of desire must remain at least a little mysterious and abstract; as intolerable as the prospect of otherness may be to the ego, it is also required for our erotic lives. As threatening as enigmatic otherness may be, too much detail is an anaphrodisiac. For the sake of sexual pleasure, a balance must be struck between specificity and abstraction. This is less about being treated as a subject or an object than it is about being treated as an individual or a group member. For this reason, I prefer the concept of fetishization over objectification.[10]

I don't come from depraved people. The socialists I grew up around—mostly middle-class, white Americans—were all rather normal.[11] Conservatives in the US who are apoplectic about socialism don't seem to appreciate this, but I do. I've been to the homes where socialists live, mostly in nuclear families that eat dinner together, sitting around a table or in front of a television. I've met the socialist parents who work in education, social work, law, and medicine, and who care about their kids' grades and friends. I've been to the socialist barbecues where "world music" is played at a reasonable volume, and adults drink bottles of beer and wine, with a basketball game on in the background. I spent more than a decade of summers at a socialist sleepaway camp in the Berkshires, swimming in a frigid lake, drinking "bug juice," and playing spin the bottle and truth or dare with pimply kids with hyphenated last names. And I've watched many of these burgeoning socialists grow up and, after a requisite period of youthful indiscretion, get married and have kids of their own, not unlike my conservative peers in suburban New Jersey.

The socialists I grew up around were not puritans, but neither were they libertines. They sowed their wild oats, but they weren't fucking strangers in back rooms and public parks. While not explicitly homophobic, many of them hardly welcomed—and sometimes openly disdained—the qualities they associated with gay men: male femininity, passivity, superficiality, laziness, self-gratification, melodrama, and licentiousness—an intolerance rooted in the dominant culture but also in their antipathy toward the bourgeoisie, with whom they linked these qualities.[12]

It wasn't until my twenties that I discovered a more depraved, more queer left, for whom daytime activism was routinely followed by nighttime hedonism—a juxtaposition of tendencies: responsible and altruistic on the one hand, and irresponsible and pleasure seeking on the other. I was ushered into this scene by my friend Craig, whom I met in grad school. Craig took me to my first bathhouse and was also with me when I got arrested at a Critical Mass bike ride protesting the Republican National Convention in 2004. To my delight, this queer left was less normal and more debaucherous than the left of my youth, with a kind of "work hard, play hard" ethos that was as committed to social life as it was to social justice. Comrades and cum rags.

I felt the kind of relief that gay Christians must feel when they finally find an accepting church. In this scene, I could be a Marxist and a pervert, integrating these core aspects of my life, neither a secret to the other. But the embrace of perversion, I would learn, was not entirely unconditional; it depended on one's ethical handling of communication, power, and conflict. You could be a slut without shame, as long as you were an ethical slut, to quote the title of a popular book on non-monogamy.[13] What initially seemed like the peaceful coexistence of left politics and queer sexuality was thus revealed to be more like an ethical battleground where sexual desires and pleasures are evaluated according to the dictates of social justice.[14]

The fetish/kink community may have garnered some social acceptance over the past few decades for those who like to kiss and caress feet, or get tied up, or give someone the spanking they deserve, but fetishizing groups of people remains a no-no for many on the left. A white-collar professor like me, for example, should not harbor a penchant for rough trade.[15] The problem with this kind of fetishizing—for those who have a problem with it—is typically that it casts (oppressed) people into preexisting roles that ignore their individuality and/or reproduce universalizing assumptions about the group(s) to which they belong, some of which may be false, hurtful, and harmful. Imposing rigid scripts, as our fantasies may dictate, doesn't help. The alternative to fetishizing someone is to appreciate their individuality, to not "reduce" them to a particular feature, while remaining open to their own articulation of identity and personhood.

This understanding of fetishism is indebted to Freud. For Freud, fetishism is exclusively a male problem. As Andrea Long Chu humorously puts it: "Classical Freudian fetishism is a kind of witness protection program for the phallus. The little boy, traumatized by the discovery that his mother has no penis, and fearing lest the same fate befall his own, supposes instead that the penis has fled her body and is now living in a flyover state under an assumed name: Foot, perhaps, or Velvet, or Panties."[16] As long as the fetish is embraced, the boy/man can avoid confronting his mother's (and all women's) difference, even though the fetish is a reminder of that original, awful scene.[17]

Taking a note from feminist philosopher Luce Irigaray, Anne McClintock suggests that what men with fetishes truly fear is not the difference materialized by women's missing penises, but rather by women's different desires; it's not the idea that women don't have penises that is so disturbing to these men, but rather the idea that women don't even want them. As Leo Bersani puts it, penis envy describes how men feel about having a penis, imagining that women must want to have one.[18]

Feminist critics have unsurprisingly rejected Freud's chauvinism and misogyny, though many still retain his notion that fetishes are compensatory objects meant to substitute for some kind of loss. As McClintock writes:

> Fetishes can be seen as the displacement onto an object (or person) of contradictions that the individual cannot resolve at a personal level. These contradictions may originate as social contradictions but are lived with profound intensity in the imagination and the flesh. . . . The contradiction is displaced onto and embodied in the fetish object, which is thus destined to recur with compulsive repetition. Hence the apparent power of the fetish to enchant the fetishist. By displacing power onto the fetish, then manipulating the fetish, the individual gains symbolic control over what might otherwise be terrifying ambiguities. For this reason, the fetish can be called an impassioned object.[19]

This analysis makes it possible to apply the theory of fetishism to all kinds of social desires—raced and classed, to take two prime examples—rather than simply gendered desires. According to this view, my attraction to working-class masculinity could be a symptom of classed and gendered anxieties. What contradiction might I not have been able to resolve at a personal level? Maybe it has something to do with my childhood femininity, entangled with feelings of shame about my family's upward mobility, inherited from my communist parents. Maybe the eroticization of working-class masculinity offers my psyche an opportunity to experience a comforting sense of control over these circumstances.

Freud was interested in the genesis of all desire, not just desire deemed "abnormal." To his credit, he saw "normal" heterosexual desire as an achievement rather than a natural development. He considered no desire more natural than another; all desire entails the repression of a fundamentally polymorphous childhood sexuality. This important point has been forgotten or ignored by many critics of fetishization, who assume that there is a better, non-fetishistic way to want people. In other words, there are proper and improper ways to want; the proper way is to desire, while the improper way is to fetishize. To want gendered others is to desire, but to want raced or classed others is to fetishize. It is for this reason that Jacques Lacan's proposal that the penis itself might be a fetish object is so powerful. Whatever the particular genesis of our different desires, they are all fundamentally equivalent in kind. As Tim Dean puts it, desire is "ineluctably fetishistic."[20] It always involves imbuing neutral objects with psychic meaning.[21] We might therefore think of fetishes, in the critical sense ("don't fetishize me"), as simply desires that people don't like: because they don't like the singling out of particular features, or they don't like the meanings ascribed to these features, or they don't like being confined to these meanings, or they take issue with whoever is doing the ascribing.

In one sense, sexual desire is always specific. We are turned on by certain qualities—certain kinds of bodies or body parts, mannerisms, ways of talking and moving, relational dynamics, sexual acts—even when these are unconscious, or when we're unable to articulate them. When we ask people about their desires (*into?*), we're essentially asking them to name this specificity. Allow me to be as specific as possible: I want to fuck Murk Ruffalo's character (Terry) in the bathtub scene in *You Can Count on Me*. But it's not really Mark/Terry's face, body, posture, demeanor, and accent that turn me on, it's their meanings. The traits that I read in Mark/Terry as working class deliver to me a kind of soft masculinity I desire. In this sense, I desire a specific person (Mark/Terry), but not as an individual. He's a conduit, a particularly useful instrument because of the particular meanings he aggregates into one package. These meaningful qualities are specific and yet, in order to be hot, he must remain abstract and enigmatic: a fetish.

Cruising is a cyclical process that tends to end after sex, not only because the itch has been scratched, but because our desire dissipates as our fetish objects become detailed and complicated. And then, sometime later, it begins again: when someone shows up at my door, across from me in the steam room, or at the urinal next to me. And before this, when we're just messaging or making eye contact. And even before this, while I'm waiting, looking around for someone who might strike my fancy—a moving target for which I will forever be searching.

Cruising is also something we do side by side rather than together, even when we are face-to-face. When I have sex with a stranger, I'm largely in my own world, pursuing my own desires and fantasies while my partner does the same. As Tom Roach writes, "We are granted the power *not* to be recognized, and not to recognize others."[22] This isn't about reciprocity but rather joint aggrandizement (an obscure notion from labor history elaborated by Jonathan Cutler): a fortunate compatibility of interests between different parties.[23] As Alex Espinoza puts it, cruising is about "two people getting exactly what they want from each other and then walking away."[24] I suspect that non-anonymous sex—that is, with dates, fuck buddies, boyfriends and girlfriends, partners and spouses—entails less reciprocity than we may be comfortable acknowledging, but cruising makes it difficult to ignore that we're all doing our own thing, pursuing our desires and reading each other for the possibility of compatibility. But compatibility doesn't mean we're on the same page. In my psyche, for example, topping and bottoming aren't linked to dominance and submission, but for many people they are. Thankfully this divergence doesn't matter as long as our desires are sufficiently synchronized. I don't need to feel dominant as a top for a bottom to feel dominated by me.

On a slow day at the spa, I had my eye on a muscular, white, middle-aged guy who was spending a lot of time alone in the sauna. His gorilla-like body, his masculine tattoos, his stoic facial expression, his swagger, the unusually large towel wrapped around his waist, and his avoidance of the steam room all read very straight to me, very biker or mixed martial arts (MMA) fighter. Cruisers at the spa almost always expose themselves in some way unless they're insecure about their size, and even then. This guy revealed little. I wondered if he had little to show, like many guys whose bulging pecs, shoulders, and biceps attempt to compensate for a small dick, or so I assume, maybe erroneously. Then I caught a glimpse of him in the shower—he was hung. No well-endowed cruiser would be so modest. And on the off chance that he *was* interested in having sex with men, I reasoned, he probably wouldn't be interested in sex with me, with my slight frame and nerdy demeanor. And if he *was* interested in me, he'd probably want to impale me on his massive cock—not my thing. But wonder of wonders, he got down on his knees and blew me in the sauna. I was almost too stunned to enjoy it.

It's rare that this kind of guy is into me; they often seem to be looking for their clone, or for an even scarier version of themselves. I'm happy to cater to those who prefer a punier, less intimidating version of themselves (for contrast?). It's even more rare when this kind of guy wants to suck or bottom, given the widespread association of masculinity with dominance and topping. Why else cultivate that John Cena look? But it's also true that regardless of whether guys who look like this want to dominate and top, they're often expected to. If you're a tall, muscular, gay man with a big dick, there's often an expectation of dominance and topping, which creates opportunities to dominate and top and to identify as a dominant top, regardless of whatever else you may desire: bottoming, submitting, flipping, or the host of other activities that don't involve anal penetration. As Phillips puts it in the context of parent-child relations: "We make ourselves out of the demands others make of us, and out of whatever else we can use."[25] Phillips suggests that our selves can be less stable and more responsive than they seem; what appears to be our depth, truth, or essence may just be a performance crafted in response to the expectations placed on us and the opportunities afforded to us. Judith Butler famously makes a similar point: there is no thing you truly are, it's all relational. I like the way that Phillips puts it:

> All those people who no longer believe in an essential self—or, indeed, in an essential anything—people who don't need the God-terms, who no longer find words like "true" or "authentic" or "real" any use, are drawn to more performative accounts of the self; they think of the "self" as a word to cover the repertoire of performances desired by them and demanded of them in a particular culture, at a particular time. This is what Irving Goffman called "the presentation of self in everyday life" and Stephen Greenblatt calls "self-fashioning"; a presentation is made, there is a fashioning, the language of artefacts replaces the language of nature. For these people there are not true and false selves; when I say that something is "not really me," I'm not saying this is against the grain, as though there is a grain

that I am; I'm saying that for a variety of reasons I don't want to be or do whatever it is. I can't be anything I want, but there is more to me than I know.[26]

For the record, I can imagine many reasons why guys who like to bottom might want to present masculinely, despite the confusion this may cause for their objects of desire: because they want to attract even more masculine guys to top them; because gender normativity helps them stay closeted or discreet; because violating masculinity is more pleasurable the more masculine you are; because they understand bottoming as an endurance sport, and this is part and parcel of their masculinity; because they feel attractive when they resemble the kind of guy who turns them on; because they enjoy the kind of attention they attract for it; or simply because it comes easily to them.

What did I really know about the MMA guy, after all? Maybe I was his type, or his least bad option that day. Maybe he got off on our difference, or the idea that I envied him or was overcome by my attraction to him. Maybe he was indiscriminately horny. Or maybe he was reacting to an opportunity that spontaneously presented itself in the moment; one thing simply led to another. As Louis Althusser paraphrases Blaise Pascal: "Kneel down, move your lips in prayer, and you will believe."[27] I can't deny that I'm curious to know. Then again, when it comes to sex, knowing isn't really the point.

4

Masc for Masc

Blue-collar guys are hot to me, and so are their trappings. Between the presumed masculinity of the working class, the left's boner for labor, my early exposure to the films of John Hughes, and getting bullied by guys who could have starred on *Jersey Shore*, my desire has been overdetermined. I'm not saying that the proletariat isn't exploited, just that they're also sexy. Workers of the world, undress!

I like a man in muddy or greasy jeans (farmer, construction worker, mechanic), but I love a man in uniform, especially a delivery guy. I blame the suburbs, where life is lived mostly in private, behind closed doors, and where an isolated gay adolescence nurtures a rich fantasy life. Who knows what could happen when a strange man shows up at your home with a package or a pizza—just a few steps from your bedroom. And then, just a few minutes later, he'd be gone.

Case in point: a few years ago, I got head from a FedEx guy. He was in his twenties, white, smooth, and chubby. I wish I could say that I seduced him at my door, but what actually happened was that he showed up on my Grindr grid while delivering a package to a neighbor in my apartment building. I offered him a glass of water—a silly way to get him in my apartment without promising sex—and we made small talk in my kitchen. He seemed reserved, but was probably just trying to move things along; less talking, more doing—he was on the clock, after all. His terse replies to my questions made me second-guess his attraction to me, and then it started to seem like nothing was going to happen after all. We ran out of chitchat. He said he should probably get back to work. I walked him to the door, and he asked about the size of my apartment. "Do you want to see the upstairs?" I asked.

I was surprised by his aggression when we kissed, the way he pressed his body into mine. I had to take a step back, bracing myself to meet his force with resistance. I like guys with meat on their bones, though it can make for uninspired wrestling, given my weight class. He was wearing a work-related earpiece that wrapped around his head and snaked down his shirt. He unhooked the device from his body and laid it on the bed. I was surprised that I'd never noticed a delivery guy wearing such a device, in all my years of ogling them. He didn't take off his uniform, maybe because he was short on time, or because he was embarrassed about his body or his dick, which I felt—small and hard—through the synthetic fabric of his uniform pants.

After kissing for a minute, he undid the button of my jeans and lowered himself to the floor. Sucking dick is generally considered to be a submissive act, though some guys are aggressive about it, as this guy was. As Tim Dean muses, "Sucking represents a way of converting the passive position of being penetrated into an active position, or possibly a way of equivocating the distinction between active and passive."[1] The FedEx guy seemed overcome by his desire to suck, as if nothing short of asphyxiation would satisfy, his eyes welling up with tears. I imagined that he was proud of his fortitude and stamina. I sat down on the bed, passively enjoying. Some guys like to grab, hold, or guide their partner's head during fellatio, but I feel awkward doing that. Some guys who top prefer their partner to be recalcitrant—where's the fun in dominating a doormat?—but resistance from a guy who's bottoming makes me feel intolerably undesirable.

After it was over, as he was leaving my apartment he muttered, "What a fantasy." Until that moment, it didn't occur to me that we might share the same fantasy in opposite roles.

There are many gay men who, like me, eroticize masculinity. Unfortunately for us, it's relatively rare to find masculinity that feels effortless among men who have sex with men (MSM), especially gay men. And the impression of effortlessness, unfortunately, is part of the charm, hence our lust for masculine straight men—even when we don't find them particularly physically attractive—loathe as we may be to admit it. I could be wrong about this, but if I'm right: kind of tragic.

What an excellent market this situation creates for masc guys who like femme or genderqueer guys. As for the rest of us doomed worshippers of masculinity, I suppose we might try to transform our desire, a kind of pragmatic (rather than moralistic) conversion therapy. If you can't be with the one you love, honey, love the one you're with. We might also tinker with our own gender presentations, deepening our voices, uncrossing our legs, and tucking our pinkies back in. This seems to be the more popular approach to navigating the masc-for-masc market, given the intractability of desire. As Dean and Christopher Lane write, "At the level of the unconscious, sexuality is as immune to education and political domestication as it is to social discipline."[2] This is not to say that we were "born this way," or that our desire can't change, but that change is often unpredictable and outside of anyone's control.

I suspect that this conundrum is a primary motivation for cruising. As David M. Halperin notes, "The love-object has to be able to accommodate the fantasy of butch desirability that the would-be lover projects onto it. Familiarity—and gay recognition in particular—may spoil that accommodating blankness."[3] If the anonymity of cruising initially served to protect closeted or discreet men from persecution, with anonymity comes the opportunity for personal transformation; in this case, the amplification of masculinity and muting of femininity.[4] You be masc for me, and I'll be masc for you, and as long as neither of us speaks, we can both get off.[5]

What would the Grindr grid look like if you could easily attract masc guys without also donning the costume yourself? Would there be a single beard or bicep left to gawk at? This is also true of gay bars and clubs, where guys wear baseball caps and grip bottles of beer, scowling and silent. There is a lot pageantry in all this masculine preening. Browsing through tough-guy smirks and gym-mirror selfies on Grindr, I play detective, scrutinizing guys' performance of masculinity for traces of femininity: tweezed brows, coiffed hair, pursed lips, prim posture. This is less about discovering who they really are than getting a sense of what they'll be like in person.[6] Will the masculine qualities that turn me on stand up to the scrutiny of a face-to-face encounter? Will they be accompanied by feminine qualities I find unattractive? In an analysis of "straight-acting"—a descriptor sometimes used by gay men on dating and hookup sites and apps—Robert Payne employs the term "passing" to describe the ability of non-masculine men to "simulate" masculinity, while also recognizing that the ability to pass might threaten the authenticity of those qualities being simulated.[7] What other terms might we use to describe our performances that recognize their variation—and their varied reception by others—while not relying on a framework of the real thing and its copy?

Like many gay men, a gay friend of mine was bullied for being feminine when he was a kid. When he first told me this, I found it hard to believe, not because it's unusual, but because I can barely detect even the faintest trace of femininity in him now. He worked hard to transform himself, first muting and then erasing the feminine ways of talking, gesturing, and moving that had made him a target. He learned which songs were acceptable to sing along to in public, and which should be indulged in private. What started out as a conscious performance gradually became second nature. Halperin references a few guides published in the 1970s and 80s designed to help feminine gay men butch up, presumably for the purpose of getting laid.[8] Ten thousand hours of practice might be all it takes, according to Malcolm Gladwell (or Louis Althusser, absent the specific figure).[9] I'm reminded of a passage from Edouard Louis's memoir *The End of Eddy*: "I wasn't the tough guy that I wanted to be. And yet I understood that living a lie was the only chance I had of bringing a new truth into existence. Becoming a different person meant thinking of myself as a different person, believing I was something that I wasn't so that gradually, step by step, I could become it."[10] In other words, fake it till you make it.

Of course, not all MSM want to be masculine or to fuck masc guys. As Halperin succinctly puts it, "Drag queens do not lack boyfriends."[11] Another gay friend of mine who is much less masculine and more feminine went on a date with a guy who requested that he act even more femininely. My friend said that this was surprisingly harder to do than butching up—surprising because exaggerating his familiar, feminine tendencies should have been easier than acting in a masculine way that felt like more of a stretch. If only for the sake of variety, I like the idea that some MSM are immune to the allure of lumberjacks, firefighters, and construction workers. I grow skeptical, though, when Grindr users' lists of turn-ons and turn-offs read like political manifestos. It's not just the convenient alignment of one's desires with one's politics that I find suspicious, but also the need to broadcast this alignment. Being good is clearly not always its own reward.

Popular and academic conversations about masculinity in the US are now dominated by discussion of its "toxic" forms. As Maya Salam wrote in the *New York Times* in 2019, "The concept [of toxic masculinity] has been around forever. But suddenly, the term seems to be everywhere."[12] Musicians began talking about it, the American Psychological Association began talking about it, even advertisers started taking notice (Salam references a Gillette ad that uses the term). And then the *New York Times* started talking about it. In the 2020s, toxic masculinity is thought to include a portfolio of undesirable qualities: a propensity for aggression, violence, and entitlement; a disdain for femininity, including the expression of particular emotions; misogyny and homophobia; unbridled narcissism; and an obsession with power, social status, and sexual prowess. All bad things.

Where did the term "toxic masculinity" come from? Criminologist Michael Salter notes that, contrary to popular belief, the term did not originate in the feminist movement, but rather in the New Age men's movement of 1980s and 90s.[13] The men who participated in this movement aimed to recover what they thought of as "deep" or "warrior" masculinity—associated with Indigenous Americans—from so-called toxic masculinity. The problem, according to these men, was societal: Boys were being increasingly feminized, causing them to grow into frustrated and aggressive men. The short-term solution: Organizing groups of men to hike into the woods together to drum and chant.

Predictably, many conservatives reject the very idea of toxic masculinity. Or rather, they don't seem to understand that only particular forms of masculinity have been targeted as toxic. For example, in a 2017 interview, "proud Western chauvinist" Gavin McInnes told a journalist, "There's a real war on masculinity in this country that starts in kindergarten and goes all the way to adulthood. And it's not natural."[14] Fox News host Laura Ingraham agreed: There is a "war on men," fueled by a "theory of toxic masculinity" that is "infecting our lives."[15]

This is hardly surprising. What is surprising is that some critics on the queer left are similarly uninterested in distinguishing toxic from so-called "positive" masculinity, at least when it comes to white, middle-class, gay, non-trans men's eroticization of masculinity.[16] As Dean observes, "The critique of the [gay] clone—that it perpetuates an exclusionary ideal of masculinity—comes from the gay left as well as the antigay right: whereas the latter sees in sameness a narcissistic disavowal of difference, the former often regards the clone's idealization of butch, self-sufficient masculinity as a racist, misogynist, and ultimately homophobic formation."[17] The gay eroticization of male masculinity might even be as noxious to some queer critics as it to some hetero homophobes.[18]

For example, in a critique of Andrea Long Chu's book *Females* (the thesis of which is that "everyone is female, and everyone hates it"), Jack Halberstam writes:

> If you think we are all female and we all hate it, you should look up the Jewish prayer where men thank God every day that they are not born female. You should then visit a gay bar where trans men are not particularly welcome, and ask if we are all female and we all hate it. You should go over the details of the various sex scandals engulfing men like Jeffrey Epstein, Bill Cosby, Harvey Weinstein, and others who love being male. You should also take a look at Grindr where men advertise for real men, males, "no sissies, no fats, no Asians." And, of course, no females. Ever.[19]

Leaving aside Halberstam's odd misreading of Chu—each of these examples seems precisely to confirm her argument that "human civilization represents a diverse array of attempts to suppress and mitigate femaleness"—this passage surprised me with its brazen juxtaposition of Epstein, Cosby, and Weinstein with gay men who want to fuck only masc men; just a motley crew of misogynists, Halberstam suggests.[20]

To take another example, in her article "Heterosexuality without Women," Greta LaFleur analyzes the photograph of Pete Buttigieg and his husband, Chasten Glezman Buttigieg, which appeared on the cover of *Time* in May 2019.[21] LaFleur muses: What if these gay men aren't homonormative—the obvious critique—but actually just heterosexual. Wait, what?

Like LaFleur, I'm irritated by desexualized representations of gays and queers that are designed to convince homophobes that (gay) love is (like straight) love, as if this were the primary sticking point and not, as Bersani puts it, the image of a "grown man, legs high in the air, unable to refuse the suicidal ecstasy of being a woman," or of a woman with no desire for cis dick, and maybe with a dick of her own.[22] Of course, these kinds of sex are the primary problem, hence the redirection from sodomy to love. However, the issue for LaFleur is not just this desexualization but also, like Halberstam, the apparent absence or disavowal of women and femininity from some kinds of male homosexuality—a characteristic that is difficult to critique without seeming homophobic; if only it could be redescribed as something more easily vilified in queer discourse, like heterosexuality.

Halberstam and LaFleur might be heartened to know that it's not hard to find men on Grindr, at least in major metropolitan areas, who also ridicule the guys who write "masc for masc" in their profiles. Admittedly, some "masc for masc" guys aren't doing themselves any favors by expressing their desire for masculinity in a way that is unnecessarily shaming and hurtful, for example: "I am NOT into men that look, sound or act like females. I am a man, you should be too." But "masc for masc" can also easily coexist with an attitude of indifference or nonsexual affection for femininity. As Halperin argues, the tension between gay men's eroticization of masculinity and our cultural attachment to femininity is constitutive of contemporary gay life.

To take a final example, in a conversation published in *The New Inquiry*, Billy-Ray Belcourt links topping with masculinity, using a critique of the latter to vilify the former. He states, "In a homonormative semiotics of sex, topping is an enactment of gender; it is a performance of masculinity, which is bound up in the erotic life of whiteness."[23] Belcourt understands bottoming, in contrast, as an ethical "reach[ing] out to others." If it weren't already clear that masculinity is a problem, connecting it to whiteness (and settler colonialism, later in the interview) should remove any trace of doubt.

Lesbian masculinity, trans male masculinity, nonbinary and genderqueer masculinity, non-white masculinity, and working-class masculinity tend to receive a more sympathetic treatment by the queer left. See, for example, Kerry Manders's article in the *New York Times* about butches and studs. As Manders quotes butch author Casey Leggler, "We exist in this realm of masculinity that has nothing to do with cis men."[24] Or as Halberstam puts it in *Female Masculinity*: "Far from being an imitation of maleness, female masculinity actually affords us a glimpse of how masculinity is constructed as masculinity."[25] In distinguishing between dominant and alternative masculinities, Halberstam ensures that the kinds of masculinity he values are not contaminated by their proximity to masculinity's malignant (white, middle-class, cis) forms.

I suspect that the white, middle-class, gay, non-trans male eroticization of masculinity is irksome insofar as it feels like an endorsement, if only tacitly, as if desiring were the same thing as valuing. I also have it on good authority that the shame of one's politically troubling desires can augment their pleasure. Perhaps the politically righteous are just hedonists in disguise, whether bearded queer critic of masculinity or anti-gay politician caught cruising public restrooms. As Adam Phillips writes, "The forbidden coerces desire. It makes something strangely alluring. It may make us obedient, but it also makes us dream (often at the same time). To abide by a rule you have to have in mind what it would be to break it."[26]

༄

This might all sound a bit defensive, like I'm calling for the queer left to distinguish between toxic and positive masculinity so that they might understand that not all gay men who eroticize masculinity are bad (that is, because we desire and/or embody the positive forms). The other typical defensive response is to find something good—politically revolutionary, psychologically therapeutic, ethically exemplary, or socially benevolent—in the bad thing. While I'm tempted to offer a defense along these lines, or else to make the case that the gay desire for masculinity is no worse than any other desire, I prefer Bersani's approach. Bersani resists the defensive impulse to sanitize queerness and thereby appease the cops and pearl-clutchers. Make no mistake, Bersani says, gay bathhouses are characterized by competition and hierarchy, not democracy. And S/M doesn't subvert power differences, it advertises their erotic charge. And the gay desire for beards and biceps isn't about subverting masculinity, but rather worshipping it.

Bersani does ultimately embrace bathhouses and S/M, but precisely for their unsavory qualities, not because they're bastions of liberal democracy. Writing during the reign of the so-called "gay clone," a masculine ideal made possible by gay liberation, he is less enthusiastic about masculinity:

> The dead seriousness of the gay commitment to machismo . . . means that gay men run the risk of idealizing and feeling inferior to certain representations of masculinity on the basis of which they are in fact judged and condemned. The logic of homosexual desire includes the potential for a loving identification with the gay man's enemies. And that is a fantasy-luxury that is at once inevitable and no longer permissible. Inevitable because a sexual desire for men can't be merely a kind of culturally neutral attraction to a Platonic Idea of the male body; the object of desire necessarily includes a socially determined and socially pervasive definition of what it means to be a man.[27]

In this passage, Bersani proposes that gay men—prototypically speaking—are not just attracted to the non-trans male body, but to a particular set of masculine meanings commonly associated with this body. More provocatively, Bersani argues that gay male desire coalesces through the internalization of a particular "oppressive mentality"—the "loving identification with the gay man's enemies."[28] Put another way, one becomes a gay man, in part, by eroticizing the kind of masculinity that despises homosexuality; to be gay is to want to fuck the thing that wants to destroy you. Being a gay man might thus be less about desiring masc men, per se, than it is about an attraction to a particular kind of self-destruction.

If this "inevitable" attraction is no longer permissible according to Bersani, it's because the AIDS crisis in the US unleashed a torrent of homophobic sentiment that threatened to bring to fruition gay men's destruction. He writes, "An authentic gay male political identity therefore implies a struggle not only against definitions of maleness and of homosexuality as they are reiterated and imposed in a heterosexist social discourse, but also against those very same definitions so seductively and so faithfully reflected by those (in large part culturally invented and elaborated) male bodies that we carry within us as permanently renewable sources of excitement."[29] Bersani too is a critic of masculinity, though for politically strategic reasons. For homophobia to end, men must end. This means that gayness (as we know it) must also end; it can't survive the dismantling of hegemonic constructions of maleness. Perhaps this makes Bersani oddly homophobic, though paradoxically in the service of combating homophobia.

The famous Groucho Marx joke seems apt here: "I don't want to belong to any club that will accept people like me as a member."[30] If you desire only people who are unavailable to you, your ego might need a little bolstering. Or, in the language of self-help: We accept the love we think we deserve. When gay men desire men who are unavailable, particularly masculine, heterosexual (or "straight-acting") men, the diagnosis has often been "internalized homophobia." I think this is what Bersani is getting at when he refers to the gay man's "identification with a murderous judgment against him"; homosexuality, in this framework, might be nothing more than internalized homophobia.

Bersani proposes that this identification might be "demolished" not through pride—adopting a healthy gay identity by embracing our feminine qualities—but rather by "self-shattering." To be certain, in "Rectum," Bersani characterizes self-shattering as an aspect of all sexuality, hence his assertion that "sexuality . . . may be a tautology for masochism."[31]

But there is something particularly important about the self-shattering that occurs through male bottoming because of the way it undoes the male ego. It's not that gay men bottom for the purpose of extinguishing our maleness, but rather that the pleasure of bottoming lies in this self-shattering. If you're not into psychoanalytic theory, the idea that bottoming is pleasurable because it shatters the male ego might be a tough sell. For one, it involves the idea that pleasure is not simply physical. I confess that I once asked a self-identified "total bottom" friend of mine whether he doesn't enjoy the physical sensation of topping even just a little bit. His answer: no. Of course, there are other reasons one might be critical of the idea that bottoming is self-shattering: Male subjectivity is differently constructed depending on race and other social factors; one can be a bossy bottom; bottoming can confirm rather than challenge the male ego when understood as a test of resilience, and so on. I think Lauren Berlant's response (as recalled by Gila Ashtor) is the funniest: "Yeah, but then you get up and go to the fridge and get a banana."[32]

For Bersani, internalized homophobia is thus not something to be overcome through therapeutic self-reckoning. In fact, its presence might be required to experience the ecstasy of self-shattering. Bersani often makes this kind of move in his writing: we can't get rid of the "bad" thing. Someone needs to top in order for someone else to bottom. One needs a self in order to self-shatter. This makes Bersani different from other critics. Rather than deconstructing antagonistic pairings, Bersani preserves them. I wonder if deconstruction appeals as a method to critics who find it difficult to tolerate conflict.

Still, Bersani's argument can read like an inversion of the gay obsession with dick, not unlike the queer left's distaste for white, non-trans men's eroticization of masculinity. The "proud subjectivity" of which Bersani is highly critical is, after all, a "masculine ideal," and the self that "swells with excitement at the idea of being on top" is a particular problem for those whose "sexual equipment" facilitates the "phallicizing of the ego."[33] His argument thus suggests that topping is politically tolerable only on the condition of versatility: an altruistic sacrifice that MSM make so that we can take turns experiencing the ecstasy of eviscerating our maleness. Bottoming, in turn, is valued as a way of preventing our desire for masculinity from nurturing within us a conservative, identitarian animus. As Bersani astutely observes, "Right-wing politics can . . . emerge quite easily from a sentimentalizing of the armed forces or of blue-collar workers, a sentimentalizing which can itself prolong and sublimate a marked sexual preference for sailors and telephone lineman," hence the popular speculation that some of history's most bloodthirsty dictators and warlords have been closeted.[34]

Perhaps in recognition of this inversion, Bersani later qualifies his embrace of self-shattering: "Much of this now seems to me a rather facile, even irresponsible celebration of 'self-defeat.' Masochism is not a viable alternative to mastery, either practically or theoretically. The defeat of the self belongs to the same relational system, the same relational imagination, as the self's exercise of power; it is merely the transgressive version of that exercise."[35] *Even irresponsible.* I think I prefer the earlier Bersani, who advocated for moving "irresponsibly among other bodies." I wonder if Bersani too grew tired of or allergic to conflict.

There are so many twists and turns in "Rectum" that it's easy to forget that Bersani's primary concern is homophobia. This concern may no longer resonate as it once did for queer readers, given the increased political and financial power of mainstream gay organizations, the success of these organizations in fomenting movements to normalize gayness through inclusion in major social institutions (family, marriage, media, military), the diversification of gender identity, which has opened up new pathways for sexual desire, and what Ashtor identifies as the "'self-critical' turn in queer studies."[36] More than two decades after Lisa Duggan coined the term "homonormativity," being a gay man—especially a white, able-bodied, middle-class, masculine-presenting, American, non-trans gay man—can seem relatively conservative and safe, or even boring, tacky, or anachronistic, at least in places with sizable queer populations.[37] Homophobia is hardly dead in the US, as evidenced by the "Don't Say Gay" law in Florida and the mass shootings at Pulse and Club Q, among other acts of legal, social, economic, discursive, and physical violence—but homophobes aren't exactly coming for gay men like they used to.

I appreciate that Bersani's politics here are motivated by self-interest rather than ethics; whether or not one agrees with the various facets of his argument, it's not moralistic.[38] I also appreciate his willingness to recognize "the gay commitment to machismo," despite the political discomfort this may cause. That said, I question Bersani's idea that gay men are constitutionally attracted to our own destruction, not because this is a depressing idea (though it is) or because it could be used to pathologize gay desire (though it could be), but because my desire feels more productive to me than this—though I was a feminine child, and I did fail at masculinity in many ways, and I did eroticize my bullies. I wanted nothing more than for Jon Frank—a jock who sat in front of me in science class in the ninth grade, and who turned around during a group exercise to whisper in my ear, "I can smell your pussy"—to put his money where his filthy mouth was, and I suspect that some part of him wanted the same. I'm not sure how to understand my desire, but "loving identification with the gay man's enemies" doesn't feel quite right.

꿏

In an interview, Andrea Long Chu states, "*Everyone* should be allowed to want things that are bad for them"—allowed, presumably, without being shamed or otherwise sanctioned.[39] While I agree with Chu, I bristle against the defensiveness of this statement, which suggests that desires need to be allowed. There are other things I'd like to say about the gay desire for masculinity, other than "I'm sorry, it is a little misogynist," or "Not all forms of masculinity are toxic," or "I love my femme sisters, I just don't want to fuck them," or "It has nothing to do with heterosexuality, I swear," or "Aren't there more important things to pay attention to in the world?" Once again, the defensive posture can get in the way of apprehending nuance, complexity, and heterogeneity.

Is there not something delightfully twisted about wanting to fuck your bully? It might be the least intelligible response to having been threatened, degraded, and humiliated. A desire for revenge or punishment would make sense, as would the more therapeutic response: reckoning, apology, and healing. But arousal?

My friend Rachel—whom I met in grad school, and who left sociology to become a psychoanalyst—once observed that there are Marx people and Freud people. The Marx people believe that humans have the capacity to be better; they're the fixers, the organizers. The Freud people believe that humans are hopeless and would be better off just accepting that we're a mess and getting on with our lives. As Eugene Thacker puts it, "We didn't really think we could figure it out, did we?"[40] I can't deny that I feel pulled in both directions.

Privileged gay men who might otherwise be apolitical sometimes become Marx people because they were bullied, socially excluded, tormented at home, or denied access to needed resources on account of their sexuality or femininity. They might also be in the market for a new congregation, or a sense of common purpose or meaning, or a respectable venue for their anger and frustration. For me, raised by communists, politics was a family affair. If anything, my experiences with homophobia kindled my Freudian side; I always wanted to fuck my bullies more than I wanted to enlighten, punish, or be rid of them.

There is a scene in Stephen King's novel *It* in which one of the main characters—a tween girl named Beverley—accidentally stumbles upon a group of bullies hanging out at a local garbage dump. Hiding in a junked car, Beverley watches them with curiosity and dread. Two of the boys in the group eventually leave, and two are left: Henry, the ringleader, and Patrick, who kills small animals and keeps their corpses in an old refrigerator—the young sociopath's calling card.

> "Let me show you something," Patrick said.
> "What?" Henry asked.
> "Just something." Patrick paused. "It feels good."
> "What?" Henry asked again.
> Then there was silence.
> *I don't want to look, I don't want to see what they're doing now, and besides, they might see me, in fact they probably will because you've used up all your luck today, girly-o. So just stay right here. No peeking . . .*
> But her curiosity had overcome her good sense. There was something strange in that silence, something a little bit scary. She raised her head inch by inch until she could look through the Ford's cracked cloudy windshield. She needn't have worried about being seen; both of the boys were concentrating on what Patrick was doing. She didn't understand what she was seeing, but she knew it was nasty . . . not that she would have expected anything else from Patrick, who was just so weird.
> He had one hand between Henry's thighs and one hand between his own. One hand was flogging Henry's thing gently; with his other hand Patrick was rubbing his own. Except he wasn't exactly rubbing it—he was kind of . . . squoozing it, pulling it, letting it flop back down.
> . . .
> She saw that Patrick's thing had gotten a little longer, but not much; it still dangled between his legs like a snake with no backbone. Henry's, however, had grown amazingly. It stood up

> stiff and hard, almost poking his bellybutton. Patrick's hand went up and down, up and down, sometimes pausing to squeeze, sometimes tickling that odd, heavy sac under Henry's thing.[41]

Beverly wasn't turned on by what she saw, but I was. I think I was twelve or thirteen—Patrick's age—when I first read *It*. I reread this passage so many times it creased the book's spine. I intuitively understood that this behavior was meant to signal a more comprehensive depravity, as if it weren't clear enough already. Bullies, sociopaths, perverts. And yet it was still hot, in part because of the way King draws out the scene, describing it in titillating detail ("almost poking his bellybutton"). The salacious, underage homoeroticism almost makes up for the homophobia. I'm not sure who I wanted to be more: Beverley, the eavesdropping voyeur; Henry, the masculine bully suddenly made docile, queerly aroused; or Patrick, with Henry in the palm of his hand, if only for a minute or two. Why does Patrick—the instigator—remain flaccid during this encounter? I find this detail delightfully perverse. Is he not turned on? Is his arousal too queer to be legible?

℮

There is more diversity within the gay desire for masculinity than critics seems to imagine. It's reductive to presume some kind of universal masculinity; like all repositories of meaning, masculinity is culturally specific and filtered through personal experience.

What does masculinity look like to you? Does it lie in the virility of youth or the wisdom of age? Is its skin taught and soft or creased and rough? Does it have scars or blemishes? Is its chest smooth, hairy, or furry? Does it have facial hair and how is it groomed or not groomed? Is it bald(ing) or does it have a full head of hair, and what's it like: color, texture, cut, style? Is it in the shape and size of a jaw, brow, lips, nose, eyes? Does it have a particular skin color? Can you read it in a facial expression? Which emotions does it express and not express? Does it care what you think? Is it compassionate? Is it independent, stubborn, confident, bossy?

How deep is its voice? Is it loud? Can you detect it in an accent or affectation? Does it speak in a particular way, using certain kinds of words and avoiding others, forming certain kinds of sentences? Does it ask questions? Does it speak declaratively? Has it been educated? What does it know a lot about? What does it like to talk about? Or does it prefer not to talk? Does it like to argue? Does it interrupt?

What does it smell like: sweat, detergent, deodorant, cologne, aftershave, beer? How is it dressed? Does it have the feel of leather, flannel, spandex, silk, denim? Is it tattooed or pierced? Does it smoke cigarettes or cigars? What can its body do and not do? What can it tolerate or endure? How does it move and not move? What is its posture like? How tall is it? How does it carry its weight? Is its body beefy, muscular, bony, sinewy, fat? Can you read it in the shape and size of shoulders, arms, neck, chest, legs? What do its hands look like and how do they move? How do they touch?

Does it come from money or not so much? Does it live in a particular kind of place: urban, rural, apartment, house? What does its home look like? Is it kept fastidiously tidy like a military barrack, or is it in slovenly disarray? Does it drive a particular kind of vehicle? Does it ride a motorcycle, bicycle, skateboard? What does it like to eat, and in what quantities? How does it like to spend its free time? What does it prefer to read, watch, listen to? Does it own a weapon? Does it have a political party? Does it go to religious services? Is it pious?

Does it have a dick, organic or synthetic? What does it look like? Is it hard or flaccid, a bulge in briefs or a jock strap, an outline in boxers or basketball shorts? Does it have a foreskin? Does it have a pussy (front and/or back)? Does its ass/hole matter? Does it have balls? Pubic hair? What does it like to do with these parts or have done to them? How forceful is it? Does it make eye contact during sex, or are its eyes trained elsewhere or closed? Is it encouraging? Does it give orders? Does it moan or grunt? How does it like to finish?

I'm reminded of a passage in *The Argonauts* in which Maggie Nelson cites Eve Sedgwick: "*Even identical genital acts mean very different things to different people. This is a crucial point to remember, and also a difficult one. It reminds us that there is difference right where we may be looking for, and expecting, communion.*"[42] If Bersani makes a sociological point—gay men mostly desire hegemonic masculinity—Nelson is making a psychoanalytic point: Maybe we don't desire the same thing, even when it seems that way.

When I was younger, before beards and dad bods were popular, I was puzzled by what I perceived to be mainstream gay norms of attractiveness, and particularly the prizing of young, smooth, muscular bodies, clean-shaven faces, and coiffed hair. More precisely, I didn't understand how these qualities could seem masculine to other gay men. Granted, the interest in musculature kind of made sense, though the self-consciousness of bodybuilding has always seemed feminine to me; the muscles might be masculine, and the process of acquiring and maintaining them might involve enduring pain and using strength, but it's also kind of like primping, especially when done in front of a mirror.[43] Lean muscle reads to me like an adornment, an accessory, a garment that might be unzipped and removed, exposing a hotter, fatter body beneath—an implausible reversal of the advertisements for gyms, diets, drugs, and surgeries that show a fat person "before" and a toned or muscular person "after." To the extent that I find muscles attractive, it's more about bulk than strength. I'm not interested in knowing how much weight anyone can bench-press, or in watching them do it.

The kinds of masculinity I find appealing are unselfconscious and not fussy, or so they seem to me. This is the appeal of body hair—in addition to being a so-called "secondary sex characteristic"—even in conventionally undesirable places: between the brows, on the back, above the collar. I appreciate smooth bodies too, as long as they haven't been intentionally depilated, but smooth guys can't advertise their defiance of grooming norms in the same way that hairy guys can.

In addition to the heterogeneity within masculinity (or masculinities), what I'm picking up on here is that gender, as Sedgwick argues, can be theorized as two distinct, orthogonal spectrums from masculine to not masculine, and feminine to not feminine, rather than one spectrum from masculine to feminine.[44] As she puts it, some people are really gender-y—both masculine and feminine—and some people aren't very gender-y at all. Again, this is to point out that there is more complexity within the gay desire for masculinity than critics imagine.

There are many other masculine attributes that one might femininely cultivate. If your beard is patchy, you can use mascara to fill it in. I came across this advice on YouTube, but tips like this have been in the queer ether for a long time. In the 1985 edition of gay trans activist Lou Sullivan's guide, *Information for the Female-to-Male Crossdresser and Transsexual*, he advises:

> Use a small comb to brush the hairs of the eyebrows up and out toward the side of the face to make them appear fuller. Take a razor to the peach fuzz on your cheeks and chin. It may be hair, but men do not have that soft down on their

faces . . . only women do. So shave it. It'll look like you just got a really close shave, plus your skin will feel somewhat rougher. If you look extremely young (and if the thought of make-up doesn't make you sick), try mascara to darken your eyebrows, but be meticulous.[45]

I may not be turned on by muscles, but there are other simultaneously masculine and feminine qualities that I find attractive, for example a certain kind of shyness that is both emotionally distant (masculine) and passive (feminine). Because of their social and historical baggage, "masculine" and "feminine" might not be the most useful terms to describe this cocktail of gendered characteristics.[46] "Masc" and "femme" might work better, not as abbreviations but as descriptors of various configurations of queer gender: the tough, taciturn, submissive ones, and the glamorous, bitchy, domineering ones.

☙

Belcourt writes that topping is generally considered to be a facet of masculinity, if not its core facet—a claim with which many gay men would agree, I think. What's a masc guy for, if not to take charge and dominate, and to be serviced by the one bottoming for him? But this is not how my desire is configured. There's something about a masc guy who loves to bottom that I find particularly hot.[47]

On Grindr, guys who want to top often send dick pics to their objects of desire, while guys who want to bottom send ass/hole pics, each advertising their wares. I'm often looking to top, but I'm not interested in ass/hole pics; few of them turn me on, and some definitely turn me off. Some guys who want to bottom for me don't seem to understand this. When I ask for a dick pic, they ask me why. They're confused: why would I care about their dick if it's not going to be crammed inside of me? My desire doesn't make sense to them, and they become suspicious. I suppose I could try to offer an explanation: I like topping masc-presenting guys, and masculinity, for me, has more to do with dicks than ass/holes. Or maybe it's because I understand erections as incontrovertible barometers of arousal, and pleasing the guy who's bottoming for me is important because it evidences our mutual attraction. Or maybe, as Bersani muses: "A man being fucked is generously offering the sight of his own penis as a gift or even a replacement for what is temporarily being 'lost' inside him—an offering not made in order to calm his partner's fears of castration but rather as the gratuitous and therefore even lovelier protectiveness that all human beings need when they take the risk of merging with another, of risking their own boundaries for the sake of self-dissolving extensions."[48] I do find it curious that bottoming doesn't compromise—in my eyes—the masculinity of my objects of desire, and may even enhance it, depending on how the sex goes. My masc fuck buddy Jeremy rarely seemed less masculine to me when he bottomed. Maybe it was the look on his face—present, eager, and confident—and the way he liked to be fucked aggressively, sometimes grunting with effort and satisfaction. He never seemed to tire or need to take a break during sex. His endurance while bottoming enhanced his masculinity to me, like a bodybuilder who invites a punch so that he can demonstrate his strength. As the joke (falsely attributed to Betty White) goes: "Why do people say 'grow some balls'? Balls are weak and sensitive. If you wanna be tough, grow a vagina. Those things can take a pounding." Ditto the ass. I'm reminded of Dean's observation that "in bareback subculture being sexually penetrated is a matter of 'taking it like a man,' enduring without complaint any discomfort or temporary loss of status, in order to preserve one's masculinity."[49] As compelling as I find Bersani's take on the gay investment in masculinity, I thus think Sedgwick was right: "Even identical genital acts mean very different things to different people," not only because of our different social positions, but also our personal histories and circumstances.

This shouldn't be news to queers for whom finding one's clone may not be the point. Dean observes that behind the sameness of "same sex" lies a world of proliferating types and endless difference, as my own desire illustrates; it's not sameness that I'm after exactly.[50]

Bersani argues that all sexual desire "combines and confuses impulses to appropriate and identify with the object of desire."[51] It's not hard to imagine how gay men express the identificatory impulse: We seek the familiarity of men and avoid the difference of women. Is this because we fear being castrated—figuratively speaking—by our fathers, so much so that we refuse to desire our mothers and, sometime thereafter, all women? This was Freud's proposition; that instead of desiring our mothers, which fills us with terror, we identify with our mothers as desiring subjects. Instead of wanting to fuck women, we end up wanting to fuck like women.

Bersani dismisses this explanation as "a 'reduction' of sexuality . . . that most self-respecting queers find both obsolete and offensive," but when I think about the way that some gay men express visceral disgust for the vulva—could this really be worse than the anus?—this explanation doesn't feel entirely off the mark.[52]

The appropriative impulse, on the other hand, might be located in feminine men's desire for "straight-acting" guys. Is this because femme gays feel insufficiently masculine and simultaneously threatened by masculinity? Do they unconsciously hope that a lover's masculinity might rub off on them, or be transferred to them through osmosis? Do they want to feel protected by masculinity, to have its power on their side for once, or to demystify its power, revealing it to be a ruse? Or do they simply enjoy lusting and pining, being frustrated and dissatisfied?

Bersani proposes that all sexual desire "combines and confuses" these impulses, but this strikes me as a particularly homo conundrum, at least when you're not your own type, because the thing that is different is also so close. As Bruce Benderson puts it, "I do believe that when one sex desires its own, there's always a touch of envy."[53] In fact, envy might be the emotion that lies precisely between identification and appropriation, sameness and difference. Envy is most acute when a desired thing is just out of reach. It's easier to lose a race by a landslide than by a split second. And while I do often feel envy for my objects of desire, something about this explanation also feels off. When I think about the pleasure of topping a masc guy, it doesn't feel like it's comfort, protection, or revenge that I'm after; not that I'm immune to wanting these things in other contexts. I may have even wanted these things from my masculine objects of desire in the past, when I was a student who regularly fantasized about a hot coach taking advantage of me (if only I'd played a sport), when my face was smooth and my hair touched my shoulders, and I was unconvinced of my own agency.

In an essay titled "Genital Chastity," Bersani amends his characterization of sexual desire in a way that better resonates with my current situation. He proposes that desire can express an appetite for what he calls "inaccurate replication."[54] While "replication" might sound close to "identification," it is modified by "inaccurate." According to this idea, rather than desiring other people because our egos are threatened by their difference, or because we're comforted by their sameness, we might desire them because we recognize in them a shared potential; we use other people as a way to bring to fruition our own desired latent potential, and they do the same to us. This isn't about who we are, or who they are, but about who we and they might become. There are no depths here, no core selves.

When I think about Jeremy's masculinity and the pleasure of topping him, I'm struck by how much I wanted to satisfy him, not unlike men who are narcissistically fixated on their ability to bring a woman to orgasm. It's admittedly peculiar, this desire to please someone in a way that they are—as a masculine man—not supposed to enjoy, but this transgression is part of what makes it hot. I didn't want to dominate Jeremy exactly, and I didn't want him to submit to me either, whether as some kind of vengeance against masculinity, or to prove my own masculinity by winning a contest for dominance, or to demystify masculinity. I did want to release something in him, I think, or to release him from something, at least temporarily; I like to fantasize that even the most masculine men might harbor a desire to be penetrated, and an ability to experience intense pleasure from it. But I also wanted Jeremy to retain his masculinity, even while bottoming. And he did retain it, or so it seemed to me, even when he was overcome with pleasure. I wouldn't call him a power bottom, exactly, but he was in the neighborhood.

When we first met, Jeremy didn't seem particularly interested in bottoming, and I was fine with that. The dynamic we created together surprised me, and I think it surprised him too. Maybe we recognized in each other something that would help catalyze a desirable transformation in and between us, as Bersani suggests. Maybe we were variations on a theme, different enough to attract each other but similar enough to make these differences feel attainable. I don't think I'll ever get to the bottom of our dynamic, of what exactly we were doing with each other through sex and why. I don't think it's possible to really know this kind of thing, though it's fun to ponder. But I'm fairly certain of this: it's an unimaginative criticism that can only understand it in terms of self-hatred, misogyny, or femmephobia.

5

Abject Objects

Cruising isn't only about finding strangers to have sex with, it's also about rejecting strangers and being rejected by them. When a cruising spot is busy, there's a lot of milling about, with guys peacocking while they rank their options, size up their competition, and ignore whoever they're not into. At the Korean spa, for example, competition for a spot in the hot tub can be intense, especially if there's a popular guy already soaking. If I have my eye on someone and he goes into the hot tub, I'll usually wait a minute before joining to avoid seeming overly aggressive or desperate. But if everyone has their eye on the same guy, I might feel compelled to pounce. And if that guy likes me too, we might have to follow each other around for a while, waiting for the right moment to engage.

Alternatively, a guy in the hot tub who nobody wants to fool around with might drive everyone away. Stalemates are not uncommon—that is, when there's room in the hot tub and a popular guy lingering nearby, but an unpopular guy or two already soaking, stubbornly biding their time. I'm impressed by the tenacity of these guys. Some try to make eye contact with every other guy in the room, seemingly confused that nobody will join them. Others will look straight ahead, stony faced, signaling their resolve. The rest of us can't exactly complain that they're monopolizing the hot tub, when there are empty seats. Sometimes a popular guy will pull a bait and switch by going into the steam room or sauna, drawing everyone else out of the hot tub—including any unpopular guys eager to join the massive circle jerk they must imagine is happening in their absence—and then returning to the newly empty hot tub.

Rejection on Grindr is typically more straightforward and often takes the silent form of no response—no gentle dismissal, no explanation, no "sorry" or "good luck!" Some guys believe they're entitled to a response. Silence frustrates or even infuriates them. They want it spelled out for them: "I'm not interested." They say that this is about "common human decency" or not being a "pussy," "dick," or "asshole"—all the dirty body parts. It's striking how quickly some guys will respond to an unanswered message with a lesson in manners and then a scathing insult. Other guys are more tenacious, even after being rebuffed. If they feel rejected or ignored, they don't show it, nor does it seem to deter them. Is it confidence or dignity that keeps them on task, or maybe the absence of these qualities? Have they learned through experience that repeated solicitation works, whether because it wears down the other person or catches them in a moment of weakness? Or maybe they're just not paying that much attention.

The first guy I had sex with from Grindr ghosted me shortly after we hooked up. Our encounter had been reasonably awkward, but I found him attractive and we were sexually compatible, so I wanted to see him again, having learned a few lessons: Wear contacts, have condoms on hand, keep small talk to a minimum, take it to the bedroom. As he was leaving my place, he said—unprompted by me—that he'd message me to let me know when he got home, which he did, but not until the next day. When I replied too quickly that I'd enjoyed meeting him, he didn't respond. Nor did he respond when I messaged him again a week later. He didn't block me on the app, and didn't need to; I got the message, so to speak.

To ghost is to reject someone without warning, explanation, or justification. It's a particularly detached form of rejection. The ease with which we can ignore other people through our screens has made ghosting more possible and, I suspect, more acceptable. It's the escape hatch some of us had been waiting for. I imagine that the ghost is the person who leaves, haunting the person left behind with their sudden, unexplained disappearance; now you see them, now you don't. Or maybe the ghost is the person left behind, feeling present but invisible. My friend Rachel (the therapist) once told me that if forced to choose between negative attention or neglect, children often prefer negative attention. This surprised me, because I so often wished to be ignored by the kids who taunted me. Then again, I had loving, attentive parents.

In an interview, 1970s gay icon Peter Berlin muses:

> I was never rejected in my life. Why? Not because I'm so cute, but because I never in my life went up to anybody and said, "I

want you." Now, I had a lot of people that I ended up having a good time with. At some point I've asked myself, "Why did I choose that person? They're not really that attractive, not really this, not really that." The first thing that comes to mind is respect. They never put me in the position to reject them. I don't want to reject anything. But when you push me, I can do it in a split second."[1]

The interviewer interjects, "That is the art of cruising: to communicate your attraction without words," to which Berlin responds: "The art of living in a community where you don't create something like rejection." But even in silence, cruising entails physical cues that signal interest; you may not say "I want you," but holding someone's gaze and grabbing your crotch communicates as much. Rejection can be as subtle as a "silent headshake," as Alexander Cheves writes, or a turn of the shoulder.[2] Maybe Berlin is describing that particular facial expression some cruisers have, that look that says, "I might fuck you, but I'm not going to chase you, and I don't want you to chase me."

To repeat a sociological truism: our desires and pleasures are social, informed by the meanings attached to bodily matter. We learn these meanings from the social worlds we inhabit. Samuel Delany put it this way: "Desire is *never* 'outside *all* social constraint.' Desire may be outside one set of constraints or another; but social constraints are what engender desire; and, one way or another, even at its most apparently catastrophic, they contour desire's expression."[3] Some kinds of body are rarely rejected, while others are rarely solicited. Some kinds of body are more widely desired than others, or are only desired in particular ways.[4] As Amia Srinivasan writes, "Consider the supreme fuckability of 'hot blonde sluts' and East Asian women, the comparative unfuckability of black women and Asian men, the fetishisation and fear of black male sexuality, the sexual disgust expressed towards disabled, trans and fat bodies. These . . . are political facts, which a truly intersectional feminism should demand that we take seriously."[5] Shaka McGlotten makes a similar point, noting that "the benefits of the [online dating/hookup] market tend to accrete to the very few—namely, well to do, young, and very often white, men."[6]

The uneven distribution of desire according to racialized gender (among other social characteristics) may be a political fact, but it's narrated here in a way that unnecessarily frames "fuckable" and "unfuckable" groups as victims. In support of these victims, Srinivasan advocates for an interrogation and transformation of our desires. She writes, "The fact is that our sexual preferences can and do alter, sometimes under the operation of our own wills—not automatically, but not impossibly either." Srinivasan's goal is a redistribution and recalibration of desire so that it is not socially discriminatory, and maybe not social at all; she seems to be proposing that we all ought to have an equal chance to be desired as individuals in a non-fetishizing way, and that none of us should be excluded from other people's field of desire on account of our social characteristics.[7]

In a 2018 conversation with Anastasia Berg, Andrea Long Chu responds to Srinivasan:

> So say someone says, "I don't like sleeping with fat, femme, or Asian guys." The implication of the critique of that is that fat, femme, and Asian guys, (1) want to be slept with by that person, and (2) that being fat, femme or Asian requires you by definition to want to sleep with people who are fat, femme or Asian. The people who are victims in the ecology of desire are assumed to have, by nature, or by virtue of their marginalized position in the structure, desires of their own which are inevitably more ethical than anyone else's. I think that is a kind of moralism that can be really insidious because it implies that there are people who are so oppressed that they are not allowed to want things that are bad for them. Everyone should be allowed to want things that are bad for them.[8]

To expand on what I take to be Chu's first point: there are other ways of narrating the plight of "unfuckables" that don't imagine them as deprived of attention they may have little interest in receiving. Chu is asking us to recognize the fact that some people don't want to be desired by those who reject them because they're not white, young, masculine, or muscular enough, whether because they find the people who reject them unattractive, or because they're turned off by their "preferences," or whatever. Why assume that the non-fat, non-femme, and non-Asian have all the power, sexually speaking, or even any power at all?

I'm reminded of something Adam Phillips writes: "Because everyone has had the experience of being left out—everyone, in other words, has been a child—everyone has an imagination (a provocation is also an invitation). You figure out how to get in, or you figure out what else there is."[9] Or as Samantha Irby puts it, "Maybe this is the upside of being ugly, but when men throw shit at you and scream lewd shit at you from passing cars on the street when you're just trying to get to the bus stop after school, the idea of there being one in a bespoke suit descending from a carriage to escort you to a fancy party doesn't seem like a thing that could happen in real life."[10]

All children may be left out at times, as Phillips writes, but some are more left out than others. For much of my femme childhood and adolescence, I was socially excluded and bullied: objects were thrown at me in the locker room, I was pushed against walls, "pantsed" in gym class, threatened in the hallway, called all the usual names, placed at the center of rumors of varying creativity (my favorite of which is that I had "marched in the gay parade." While not technically true, the rumor accurately captured both my faggotry and outspoken politics). I dreaded the non-academic parts of school because of this unpredictable violence and intimidation. While I don't recommend the experience, I may be better off for it in certain ways. As Heather Love writes, "By living 'an impossible existence'—of being excluded from central sites of social inclusion (the family and the couple)—queers have developed resources of negativity."[11] Love has in mind a queer "resistance to the world as given" that could motivate and inform coalitional politics, but I'm thinking here about the kinds of freedom made possible by exclusion. My inability to conform socially barred me from popularity, or even just acceptance, which meant that I had more latitude to do what I wanted and be how I wanted. I had a handful of friends—other weirdos—but I was kind of lonely and too often afraid. After a while, though, the idea of scrounging for the approval of my peers seemed not only pointless but noxious. Did they think I was envious of them? They should have been envious of me.

There is also the possibility that one might enjoy, or be enlivened by, rejection. When my first Grindr hookup ghosted me, I was disappointed because my desire had been activated by him; I had begun to fantasize. His disinterest didn't cure me of my desire, it heightened it—for a while. There can be pleasure in crushing, perhaps more so for those of us who aren't systematically rejected because of our race, gender presentation, age, serostatus, or other socially meaningful characteristics. Consider the gay male desire for heterosexual masculinity. It's possible that I desire straight men because I can never have them; my desire is motivated by exclusion. It's a desire that can never be satisfied. Do I want to be rid of it? No. At the end of her essay "On Liking Women," Chu writes: "You don't want something because wanting it will lead to getting it. You want it because you want it. This is the zero-order disappointment that structures all desire and makes it possible. After all, if you could only want things you were guaranteed to get, you would never be able to want anything at all."

Chu's second point—that we should all be allowed to want bad things—is softened somewhat by being on the side of the excluded. In other words, while Chu is arguing that we should all be allowed to want bad things, her emphasis is on marginalized groups and the ways that their desires are policed. Chu is concerned that "moralism about the desires of the oppressor can be a shell corporation for moralism about the desires of the oppressed," meaning that critics target the exclusionary desires of the privileged as an indirect way of critiquing the exclusionary desires of the oppressed.

This could be self-advocacy on Chu's part, but it also wouldn't be a difficult argument for someone on the left with pretty privilege to get behind. How compassionate for an attractive person to concede that unattractive people should also be allowed to discriminate against (other) unattractive people; just because you're ugly doesn't mean you should settle! It's also rather self-flattering. Part of imagining oneself as desirable can entail the fantasy that the excluded are deprived and want desperately to be included, even if only partially. In the film *The Devil Wears Prada*, the young ingenue Andy asks her evil boss, Miranda, "What if I don't want to live the way you live?" to which Miranda replies, "Oh don't be ridiculous, Andrea, everybody wants this. Everybody wants to be us."

I'm more interested in the touchier question of whether oppressors also ought to be allowed to want bad things. On this point Chu is a little evasive:

> I'm absolutely aware that desire is childlike and chary of government, but am I talking about a *rapist's desire*, am I talking about a *racist's desire*? Who gets to fall under that and am I prepared to take that all the way to the end? And gosh, I think it's very complicated. But! [Srinivasan] isn't really talking about whether we need to acknowledge that the rapist's desire to rape is as equally ungovernable as any other desire, though that's an important question. The easiest fix there, by the way, is to say desire and action are different things, so like you can tell someone to *do* something, but you can't tell them not to *want* something, because ontologically, it's not going to work.

As it turns out, Chu doesn't seem prepared to take this argument all the way to the end—at least not here—which would mean declaring that yes, a rapist's and a racist's desires are acceptable, or at least inevitable. She does note that there is a convenient way out of this conundrum, which is to acknowledge that moralizing desire doesn't effectively eliminate it. Moralizers may try to convince us that our desires are bad, but even if they succeed at this, our bad desires don't go away, we just become ashamed of them.

But what about the moralization of behavior? The word "want" and the clause "for them" are central to Chu's assertion that "everyone should be allowed to *want* things that are bad *for them*" (italics added). Right: What's the harm in letting people want what they want, even if their desires make them unhappy or are self-destructive? Chu isn't saying that everyone should be allowed to *do* things that are bad for them, nor is she saying that everyone should be allowed to want—or do—things that are bad *for other people*. She doesn't address the moralization of behavior.

Bad behavior is typically more objectionable than bad desire, especially when the bad behavior in question impinges on other people's well-being. It's one thing to want bad things, and another to do bad things to other people. This difference is important; it's what makes possible the idea of loving the sinner and hating the sin. For those on the left, the direction of power also matters; the determination of bad behavior depends not only on the behavior in question but also on the social locations of the offender and the target. For example, in a personal essay published in the *New York Times*, Maya Binyam defends ghosting as a means for people of color to escape the mundane, nonchalant violence of white supremacy:

> Articulating negative feelings with tact is a task most often assigned to those whose feelings are assumed to be trivial. When fear for my family—black, migratory and therefore targets of the state—is equated with the mundane anxiety of a standardized test, I find it a relief to absent myself from the calculation. Saying, without anger, "This is how you hurt me" feels routine, like a ditty, and articulating the need for isolation—"Now I intend to disappear"—is always a betrayal of the need itself. Because society demands that people of color both accept offense and facilitate its reconciliation, we are rarely afforded the privacy we need. Ghosting, then, provides a line of flight. Freed from the ties that hurt us, or bore us, or make us feel uneasy, finally we can turn our attention inward.[12]

Earlier in the essay, Binyam observes, "Those of us who neglect to disclose the seed of our indifference, or neglect to disclose the fact of our indifference altogether, are typically assumed to be selfish." For many on the left, selfishness is generally frowned upon, though it might be conditionally acceptable for groups rarely afforded the luxury, especially if their preservation depends on it. Again, the direction of power matters.

Unlike the moralization of desire, the moralization of behavior can be an effective means of social control, of getting people to do something or stop doing it, at least temporarily, for the simple reason that behavior can be surveilled and desire cannot. Anyone who has been closeted, discreet, or stealth knows this. Grindr's "community guidelines" may not be able do anything about users' discriminatory desires, but they can and do discourage users from verbalizing discrimination in negative ways: "We want you to be yourself and express yourself freely here, but not at the expense of someone else. We strongly suggest that you talk about what you are into, not what you aren't, on your profile"—as if users can't read between the lines of "masc for masc."[13]

I'm disappointed when queer people seem eager to moralize, given how often our desires and pleasures have been deemed bad. Maybe having been deemed bad for so long makes some of us even more eager to be good—albeit a different good than homophobes' good—rather than questioning how determinations of "good" and "bad" work to legitimate some desires and pleasures and delegitimate others. Or maybe it's a kind of revenge to demonstrate that we're better than our enemies. It could also be that the efficacy of moralizing makes some of us eager to try it out as a way of wielding power. No one appreciates the power of shame like those of us who have been told repeatedly from a young age that we're sick, sinful, and disgusting. Those demons tend to linger.

Moralizing can also backfire, making the forbidden irresistible, as Phillips argues.[14] One might justifiably wonder whether moralizing isn't a strategy of the unconscious to produce the pleasure of transgression, regardless of whether the forbidden thing is enjoyable on its own. In this way, moralizing inhibits our ability to experience things for ourselves and make up our own minds about how we want to live. As Phillips writes, "We do not have laws because we have desires: we have desires because we have laws."[15] I'm reminded of a story told to me by a former student: When his high school swim team traveled to competitions, they'd stay in a hotel, with teammates sharing beds. In a gesture of apparent heterosexuality, they'd build a "wall" of pillows in the bed between them. But rather than confirming their heterosexuality, this gesture seemed to evidence, if not produce, the desirability of forbidden homoerotic contact. Why else guard so vigilantly against the possibility of bodies touching? What's a little accidental nocturnal tumescence between teammates? Were they really just trying to avoid the stigma of being (mistaken for) gay? What's to worry about if everyone's on the same page about the meaninglessness of unintended contact? Could it have something to do with those little Speedos?

There are people who think that cruisers should be shamed, humiliated, imprisoned, rehabilitated, tortured, and/or killed. I don't want to know these people, be around them, hear what they have to say, answer to them, change their minds, or be subject to their aggression or violence. I suspect that most other queer people feel similarly, though it can be tough when the offenders are family, "friends," or community, or when sustained contact with homophobes is thought to be necessary for survival or social change. I don't need to think of homophobes as bad people to justify my desire to get away from them. Nor do I need to think of myself as a victim, or of homophobes as victims of a bad culture. In fact, I am suggesting that this kind of moralizing might not actually help me get what I want, just as the dictate that sex be private and intimate practically guarantees that cruising will remain popular.

Rather than declaring what people should or should not be doing, who they should or should be not excluding, how they should or should not be desiring, I'm more interested in considering how the moralization of exclusion works to produce victims and why this production might appeal to people who exercise various kinds of power or privilege. In addition to the way forbidding desire can intensify it, there is something counterproductive about normatively attractive people chastising each other for excluding "unfuckables": it evokes a paternalistic tone that reinforces the very power imbalance it claims to want to rectify, because victimhood is not meant to be arousing here. The intervention of a parent or other authority figure who forces a bully to apologize only confirms that the bully's target is, in fact, powerless (as every kid who has been bullied knows). Framing the targets of exclusion as victims thus makes it more difficult to disturb the distribution of desire, not easier. For this reason, I suspect that victim narratives can express an unconscious attachment to exclusion, which might have different motivations depending on who's telling the story.

If you want to shake up the distribution of desire, it would be more effective to change this narrative, to imagine the possibility that the excluded are already powerful. One afternoon at the spa, I was lusting after a fat, hairy, middle-aged white guy with a caveman face and a beer can dick, but he wasn't interested in me. I was disappointed, though not surprised. He wasn't conventionally attractive, but a big dick goes a long way at the spa. He eventually found his match: a young, lean, smooth Asian guy. This did surprise me, because it contradicts the popular story—repeated by Srinivasan—that Asian men are often dismissed as "unfuckable."[16] The more this story circulates, the more I expect it to be universally true, despite being a sociologist who should know better: the story is about a pattern, and individual experiences can defy patterns. Of course, I didn't know the contours of the caveman's desire—what was it about me that didn't turn him on, or about the other guy that did? Did I imagine that race was more central to my rejector's desire than it actually was? At the very least, being white didn't seem to help me, and being Asian didn't seem to hurt the other guy. This experience was instructive, because I felt the erotic value of my whiteness plummet, which underscores the way that desire can be supple, as many of us know through our waxing and waning attraction to specific other people. Desire forms and transforms through not only experience but also the circulation of stories. These stories don't simply report experience, they give meaning to it. And meaning is the currency of desire.

6

Meet Markets

People reject other people and they get rejected. They dump and are dumped, exclude and are excluded. They break up and divorce. They also simply part ways. In cruising, this typically happens after sex, if not before. At the Korean spa, I interrupt many encounters—because they are unsatisfying, because I want to delay my orgasm or pursue someone else, or because I'm overheated—by simply getting up and leaving the steam room, or floating away in the hot tub. No explanation, no insult, no polite valediction, just departure. Guys cum and go, and that's the point. Historically, or maybe just stereotypically, gay men have excelled at detachment, with our infamous allergy to commitment and our propensity for casual, anonymous sex, no strings attached. As Michel Foucault put it in an interview, "For a homosexual, the best moment of love is likely to be when the lover leaves in the taxi."[1]

According to contemporary heteronorms, it's acceptable to rebuff someone you're not into or to leave behind people who don't offer enough of what you reasonably want or need, especially if you're being mistreated or abused. But we're not supposed to be in a perpetual state of refusing or leaving; we can detach, but we're not supposed to be emotionally detached. Detachment is most palatable when narrated as part of the noble quest to find that someone special. A mature adult is supposed to be in a long-term romantic relationship with a person to whom they are responsible and vice versa. Hookups might be fine for young people, and maybe for not-young people in committed, open relationships. Someone who's been in long-term, monogamous relationships for most of their adult life might also be given a pass to fool around for a while before returning to the stability of commitment. In addition to age and relationship status, there are other sociological variables likely at play here—gender, race, ethnicity, nationality, religion, and so on—that shape the way these norms are established and applied.

As anyone versed in queer theory knows, norms are agents of social control, wrapped up in the packaging of the natural, healthy, ethical, virtuous, and well-adjusted. It is not difficult to find psychoanalytic justification for pathologizing detachment. As Adam Phillips persuasively argues, detachment can be a strategy of psychic avoidance: we sometimes detach from other people to avoid knowing or feeling things that we don't want to know or feel because we believe (not without cause) that it will disturb our identity or sense of self. In psychoanalytic terms, we repress parts of ourselves that our egos can't bear. When detaching is a strategy of avoidance, we may feel like we're moving forward by leaving someone behind, but this progress is an illusion that masks the ways we're actually stuck.

Of course, staying can also be a strategy of avoidance, depending on what we're avoiding. As Phillips writes in *Monogamy*, "Monogamists are terrorized by their promiscuous wishes, libertines by their dependence. It is all a question of which catastrophe one prefers."[2] If staying rarely gets pathologized, it's not because it's necessarily healthier, but because it's normative: staying is what we're supposed to do in the long run. We're supposed to be able to work out our problems with other people—if we're reasonable and not damaged beyond repair. The healthy thing doesn't become normative because it's healthy; the norm finds its justification in the discourse of health. Isn't that just like a norm, to masquerade as an unassailable truth so that it's more difficult to contest?

In addition to the commitment issue, cruising also touches the promiscuity nerve, which is not just about detachment but also seriality and repetition: an endless stream of sexual partners. This too can be easily pathologized using psychoanalytic concepts like neurosis, compulsion, and addiction to diagnose kinds of repetition that contradict prevailing norms. The fact that cruising is prototypically queer doesn't help its case. Homosexuality—the desire for the "same sex"—was initially linked in psychoanalytic thought to narcissism; both were understood as a perverse, neurotic appetite for the self/same.[3] There is a reason that one can be addicted to sex, but not to spending time with family, or to reading books, or to eating healthy foods; these are culturally valued activities. Having sex with one's spouse over and over is rarely framed as neurotic—even when it's a joyless, performative act—because it's what one is supposed to do. Similarly, the repetition of creating a nuclear family—like one's parents did, and their parents did, and their parents did—is also not pathologized for its seriality.

If casual sex is variably acceptable depending on one's individual circumstances and social position, it is also judged according to its specific form. There is a difference between going home with a stranger you meet in a bar, and walking into the woods on a warm summer afternoon and fucking a stranger against a tree. There might even be a difference between cruising in the woods and having sex through a glory hole, which is about as unattached as sex can get. It's so detached and anonymous that many people might not even classify it as casual sex; it's something lower, approaching the bare minimum of a sexual relationship in terms of commitment and responsibility.

It's not surprising that conservatives would take issue with this kind of detachment. Conservative *New York Times* columnist David Brooks can barely stomach the idea of online dating, which he disapprovingly characterizes as "shopping for human beings," let alone Grindr, bathhouses, and tearooms.[4] It is more surprising when scholars and activists on the queer and feminist left are made similarly uneasy by this kind of detachment, given their presumed commitment to sexual liberation. Then again, cruising is very much a market activity, characterized by impersonality and indifference, and many on the left are critical of the transactional and utilitarian nature of markets; they favor instead the responsible, bonded relations of community.[5] It's not that cruising forces users to be impersonal and indifferent to each other, but that its venues typically accommodate and facilitate anonymity and indifference, whether through a screen or in person.[6] In a meat market, everyone is essentially fungible, to use Tom Roach's term. As David M. Halperin argues, the purpose of bathhouses and back rooms is precisely "to enable us to crowd as many antisocial thrills as possible into the moment and to provide us with a structured communal space in which to heighten, express, and discharge our romantic fantasies—without doing ourselves or our partners any lasting emotional harm."[7]

It is for this reason that some on the queer and feminist left try to saddle sluttiness with ethics, nudging no-strings sex in the direction of a collective.[8] But when critics solicit cruisers to prioritize caretaking over personal pleasure, they are working against the nature of cruising, and willfully so. More to the point, they are working against the nature of sex, though cruising amplifies this "problem." As Madhavi Menon puts it, "[Desire] is indifferent, which is why it is politically incorrect."[9] This is a story with a familiar ending. As Andrea Long Chu writes, "Nothing good comes of forcing desire to conform to political principle. You could sooner give a cat a bath."[10] Working with, rather than against, the nature of cruising presents a different problem: how to build a robust market for sex, in which everyone has an abundance of desirable and viable options.

℃

Grindr has a lot of potential, in terms of manifesting abundance, though not all critics see it that way. The Grindr grid has been compared to Andy Warhol's serialized soup cans and to "an endless row of nearly indistinguishable cereal boxes at the supermarket."[11] (How did groceries come to exemplify the limitations of consumer capitalism, I wonder.) This critique might be about the way Grindr facilitates objectification, but I'd rather take it as a grievance with a lack of consumer choice. The problem, in this case, wouldn't be that we treat other people like disposable pantry items, but rather that the selection should vary more; we should have more distinguishable soup cans or cereal boxes to choose from. In the 1970s, 80s, and 90s, this critique was expressed in terms of the "gay clone" or "Castro clone." Of course, one person's abundance is another's scarcity. If I'm into whatever look is fashionable at the moment, a lack of variety might not bother me. Or rather, I might spot the differences that others miss or find uninteresting.

Grindr allows users to filter the profiles they see (by age, height, weight, etc.), presumably to search for their specific type—a process not unlike patronizing a bar or club that targets or attracts a specific demographic.[12] If you don't use filters, you see everyone (minus anyone who's blocked you, or whom you've blocked); if users seem too similar to each other, the problem—if there is one—is either that you're in a homogenous place, or that you're using the wrong app. To put it another way, if homogeneity is a problem, it's not exactly Grindr's fault, though the Grindr interface can highlight patterns in the ways people want to appear, which in turn makes it possible to evaluate and transform oneself in relation to these patterns.

Tim Dean characterizes cruising in a bar or public park as more spontaneous and livelier than cruising on an app. I don't disagree; the proof is in my elevated heart rate when I stand at a rest stop urinal or stroll through a cruisey patch of forest. But what Grindr may lack in spontaneity, it can make up for in efficiency, particularly when you know what you want and you have what it takes to make it happen. Some users may not want their sex lives to be efficient, and that's fine, but others prefer it. Grindr can be useful for facilitating sex at odd times—not only in the morning and afternoon, but while on break at work, walking the dog, waiting at the airport, or in between errands. It also makes possible encounters that might not have happened otherwise. Some Grindr users don't patronize queer venues—including cruising spots—or attend queer events. These people might be closeted, have social anxiety, be unwilling or unable to tolerate the risk of arrest, be in a monogamous relationship, not have disposable income to spend, not like the music, or not be able to physically access the space. There are a lot of "discreet" guys where I live in central Connecticut. For those of us who like to have sex with them, Grindr is a gift, as it must also be for them.

Building a robust market for sex need not be an ethical issue. As cruising spots become popular, they generate further abundance. Everyone wants to be where the action is. More cruisers means more competition, but also a greater chance of finding people to whom you're attracted, and who might be attracted to you, especially when the crowd is diverse. Put more academically, having an abundance of options can make it easier to enter into desired relations—including those that are utterly provisional, unbound, and fleeting—and to avoid or detach from unwanted relations. As Samuel Delany writes, "When so many people say 'yes,' the 'nos' don't seem so important." When I want to leave someone, or to not attach to them in the first place, it helps if I believe that I can get what I need and want elsewhere. Some relations are harder to avoid or leave than others. The harder it is for me to avoid or leave an undesirable relation, the more interested I am in figuring out ways to make leaving possible. If it's impossible for me to leave, the more I interested I am in figuring out how to gain the leverage that would enable me to minimize its toll.

From a self-interested perspective, the key to building a robust market for sex lies in creating abundance in the first place, increasing supply. Abundance is not just about filling the Grindr grid, gay bar, or bathhouse with bodies, but about desiring these bodies and being found desirable by them. What good is a room full of hot guys if none of them is interested in you, unless supplication is what turns you on? One needs currency to participate in a market. If you don't have any, it doesn't matter what you want to buy—or rent, rather. This is as true of Grindr as it is of a bar, club, or bathhouse. Abundance can thus be augmented when cruisers' field of desire expands: when we begin to find new types attractive and in a variety of ways, when our menu of desired sexual dynamics and interests grows longer, and when our libidos increase. Can this be done, especially if desire is chary of government, as Andrea Long Chu points out? Shaming people for their exclusions rarely works to expand their desire, and it can easily backfire. It might be more effective to appeal to the pleasures of a broad appetite. Again, this is to treat desire as a practical issue rather than an ethical one. It's the difference between appealing to people's moral compass and their pleasure center.

Some resources are zero-sum. Fortunately, attractiveness is not; it doesn't need to be taken away from someone to be granted to someone else. It can be multiplied. Queer scholars have often critiqued norms as regulative; norms declare who is unruly and needs to be brought into line. But there's another compelling reason to be critical of norms, particularly norms of attractiveness: they transform what could be abundance into scarcity. The narrower your types, the fewer your options.

Chu argues that "desire has to be a process of subtraction. And I think it's probably always going to be a process of subtraction. You can't want everything. It wouldn't be wanting it if it was everything."[13] Then again, Andy Warhol had a famous talent for liking everyone and everything, as Jonathan Flatley writes.[14] What a gift it would be to find pleasure everywhere, to be delighted by the variation within any given category. Is it possible to foster this kind of appreciation? I asked this question in class once, and a student responded that too much choice makes her feel unable to act. Some of us prefer fewer choices, smaller menus.

Attractiveness isn't always binary: yes or no. It's possible to find people attractive in different ways or contexts, for different reasons. At the Korean spa, some guys were made more attractive to me because of the scenario; what they looked like mattered less than what we did together, where we did it, and what else was going on at the moment. To take another example, some guys' sexual versatility is age dependent: they only want to top younger guys and bottom for older guys. The more guys that are like this, the more unfortunate it is to be a young top; it isn't appealing to be found attractive if your attractiveness depends on a dynamic you're not into.[15] Better to find people who desire you in the way that you want to be desired. Or, if there are many ways you want to be desired, better to have a portfolio of attractive suitors, each interested in a different dynamic, offering a choice: What might you want at this particular moment? This is also to say that expanding one's palette might involve not only finding more people desirable, but also learning to find people desirable in a diversity of ways.

Fantasy sometimes gets a bad rap because it is thought to hold our objects of desire hostage—"now say this, then do that"—but it can also be a way of experimenting with our objects of desire, and with expanding our desire. I like a man in uniform, but I'm not wedded to any particular script. When I fucked my local FedEx guy, I found it exciting to respond to him in real time, allowing my desire to meander down an uncertain path. Fantasy is related to imagination after all, and imagination can be supple. This is how we sometimes daydream, fantasizing about a series of different possibilities; less "now do this" than "if they do this, I might respond like that." Fantasy is sometimes dismissed as not real; there's the way you want things to be, and the way things actually are. But fantasy can be a way of appreciating the plasticity of the real.

I've stressed the importance of abundance in markets for sex, but I can't deny that scarcity has also played a role in the expansion of my field of desire. At the spa, I can't always find someone I want to have sex with, so I'll try to find someone I'm willing to have sex with. With risk sometimes comes reward. Having sex with someone I'm not particularly attracted to can feel like eating a disappointing meal when you're hungry—more utilitarian than satisfying—but I've also been also surprised by how pleasurable it can be, and by how this pleasure can transform my desire and even my relation to my desire; the more uncertain I become about who and what might bring me pleasure, the more I approach everyone as a potential source of pleasure. Unsatisfying encounters with hot guys can have a similar effect. Scarcity, then, ironically can be useful in generating new abundance.

Foucault makes a point to distinguish between desire and pleasure, privileging the latter. His privileging of pleasure over desire is a function of desire's relation to identity, truth, and what he calls biopower; pleasure is politically interesting to Foucault because it is less knowable, more superficial, and therefore less available to biopower.[16] This leads him to propose that "the rallying point for the counterattack against the deployment of sexuality ought not to be sex-desire but bodies and pleasures."[17]

Bersani implicates psychoanalysis (in its mode of unearthing repressed desires) in this critique:

> What positions, what activities, what identifications excite us? What imagined object best helps the masturbatory process along? What do we prefer the other to be doing—to us, for us, alone, with someone else? Such questions would of course not only be congenial to the confessor's forays into the penitent's soul; in more sophisticated form, they nourish the psychoanalytic curiosity about the identificatory moves of desire. The danger is clear. It is but a step from identifications to identity, and the tracing of the former's mobility may conceal an urge to find the common denominator that would, for example, definitely distinguish homosexual from heterosexual desire.[18]

It is the notion that desire is stable that makes possible this categorization. Pleasure is thought to be less stable and predictable, and therefore less manageable.

As I've discussed, there is a queer politics to resisting categorization. But somewhat more simply, I like the idea—and feeling—of being surprised by unanticipated pleasures, which is to say pleasures that don't follow from trying to satisfy a desire. We might know (or think we know) what we desire, until we're surprised by things we don't desire (or didn't know we desired) that bring us pleasure.

Another way to increase supply is to remove barriers to promiscuity: by destigmatizing and decriminalizing non-normative sex; reducing work time and expanding playtime; developing tools (like Grindr) that accommodate discretion and circumvent legal and normative restrictions; making condoms, PrEP, birth control, abortion, and STI testing and treatment free and accessible; and creating affordable and inclusive queer enclaves. These measures are all relatively uncontroversial on the left. It would be more controversial to encourage promiscuity, not because it's superior to monogamy or celibacy, but simply because of the network effect: the more promiscuous people there are, the more robust the market for sex. This could be done by nurturing a sense of sexual utopianism, a conviction that worthwhile pleasures can always be found elsewhere and ahead, and a commitment to pursuing these pleasures at the expense of monogamy, which—not to put too fine a point on it—is community writ small.

Utopianism is characterized by an optimistic orientation toward the future. Utopian thinkers believe that a better, radically different world is possible and that we have the capacity to bring such a world into being. This means that utopianism is grounded in dissatisfaction, typically directed toward social systems that produce forms of suffering and misery thought to be unnecessary and eradicable, if only we could organize the world in a different way. Because utopian thinkers typically frame our woes as systemic, they set a high bar for social change, prioritizing revolution over reform. For this reason, utopian demands—for example, the abolition of social institutions like work and the family—are often written off as impossible, and utopian thinkers are dismissed as naive. But the point of utopianism is precisely to make the impossible more possible. As Kathi Weeks argues, "A utopian demand prefigures . . . a different world, a world in which the program or policy that the demand promotes would be considered as a matter of course both practical and reasonable."[19]

I can't deny the appeal of utopianism's optimistic and stubborn refusal to settle. Maybe I just like shopping. I don't mean the activity—not that I'm opposed to it—but rather the affect: hopeful, hungry, eager for the new, and unsure of the forms it might take. This facet of my parents' political ideology intrigued me as a child. I wanted to know what things would be like after the revolution, but either they didn't know, couldn't explain it to me, or I didn't understand. We were atheists, but this desire for a future free from social, political, and economic conflict, a just and peaceful future that you could only believe in because you would never see it come to pass, now strikes me as somewhat religious, like that other "no place" in the sky. This might also be what some of us want out of therapy: an end to psychic turmoil, to be healed and whole. Will we ever find out what's buried in our unconscious? Will we ever experience the satisfaction of a life in which our desires are not repressed? Even the ascetic, quasi-Buddhist, self-help discourse now popular among middle-class white people in the US, which tells us that all the answers can be found within ourselves—like poor, exhausted Dorothy who needed only a few magic words (and those bedazzling shoes) to return to her beloved Dust Bowl—seems fueled by a suspicion that happiness or satisfaction lies elsewhere, albeit in some other part of ourselves, hiding in plain sight.

But utopianism can also mask a profound conservatism that is less about imagining a radically different state of affairs and more about preserving the status quo. José Esteban Muñoz's *Cruising Utopia*—arguably the most well-known and influential contemporary queer utopian text—appears to be thoroughly invested in a revolutionary break from the present. As Muñoz writes, "The here and now is a prison house. We must strive, in the face of the here and now's totalizing rendering of reality, to think and feel a *there and then*. Some will say that all we have are the pleasures of this moment, but we must never settle for that minimal transport; we must dream and enact new and better pleasures, other ways of being in the world, and ultimately new worlds."[20] Muñoz's characterization of "the pleasures of this moment" as a "minimal transport" is reminiscent of Marx's famous characterization of religion as the "opioid of the masses"—drugs being one way the proletariat temporarily escape the misery of alienation, oppression, and exploitation, and religion being another. Given the queer focus of *Cruising Utopia*, it is reasonable to assume that Muñoz is also thinking of sex as a pleasure of the moment.[21] There is something that can feel intensely "here and now" about the pleasure of sex, even as sexual desire has much to do with our past.[22] Sex can also feel like a kind of transport, taking us away from the "here and now," or rather from the "prison house" that is the "here and now" much of the time. Is this transport "minimal," as Muñoz writes of pleasures of the moment? If so, wouldn't it be wiser to pursue instead the "new and better pleasures" he seductively references, whatever these may be?

In a revealing passage, Muñoz cites a scene from Samuel Delany's memoir *The Motion of Light in Water*, in which Delany recounts his shock upon seeing for the first time a huge gathering of men having sex in a gym-sized room at the St. Mark's Baths. Muñoz is not interested in this licentious, debaucherous orgy, but rather in Delany's realization, in this moment, that gay men are a sizeable population and, as such, could wield political power.[23] A lot hangs on this "could," especially if wielding political power requires turning an "undulating mass of naked male bodies, spread wall to wall," as Delany observes, into an organized, collectively minded group. There is a big difference between a shared perversion and a community, an orgy and a protest.[24] As I've suggested, these need not be mutually exclusive. But for some perverts, the discipline, active disposition, and collective orientation required by political subjectivity may be inimical to their sexuality. I suspect that it is these "solitary perverts" that Muñoz has a problem with when, inspired by Delany, he writes, "[Queer] power can be realized only by surpassing the solitary pervert model and accessing group identity"—as if solitariness, rather than sociability, were the primary relational mode of the pervert. This injunction to access group identity—justified by the "new worlds" that require our collective imagination and effort to be enacted—is thus geared toward policing perverts whose predilection for detachment will always be a problem for communitarians like Muñoz, even if ambivalently. In this way, Muñoz's critique of the "solitary pervert" as a failed collective subject is "not so distant from more explicitly conservative condemnations of homosexuality as inimical to the reproduction of the social," as I argued in *Antisocial Media*.[25]

This is not to imply that collective politics is necessarily a joyless affair whose only purpose is to cement group solidarity and sanction outsiders. My activist friends get a lot out of their political work, even when their utopian visions go (as of yet) unrealized: They build fulfilling relationships by working collaboratively with others who care about the same issues; they expand their social networks and interact in enjoyable ways with a more diverse group of people than they might otherwise; they develop a sense of liveliness and adventure when they take risks and step out of their comfort zones; they experience ego-gratifying pride in their leadership and satisfaction when their campaigns and actions are successful in various ways; they come to feel a meaningful sense of connection to the places in which they live; and, of course, they feel morally or ethically good about trying to do the right thing. Needless to say, most of them are extroverts, hence our chemistry. At the same time, few of them would deny that it's a lot of work: organizing, advocating, protesting, and fighting (sometimes physically), all of which can take a toll. Without underestimating the enjoyment that activism can entail, I question whether this toll isn't only a necessary cost, but also another means of forging desired social bonds. I'm suggesting, in other words, that shared suffering can bring people together in particular ways they may (or may not) desire. The further away revolution feels to me, the more I wonder about this function.

I'm not trying to yuck anyone's yum. I have considerable respect for the people I know who pursue their political ideals thoughtfully and with compassion and humor. I also sometimes feel moved to participate in collective political action myself. But while I may be too neurotic to be a full-fledged libertine and too submissive to disavow fully the political faith in which I was raised, I'm beginning to suspect that I'm just not cut out for the revolution. There is a substantial part of me that is unavailable to a communitarian ethos. It's the introverted, irresponsible, flighty, passive, superficial, libidinous, and hedonistic part, for which the pleasures of this moment are not minimal, but rather the ultimate transport, not only from the drudgery of work, the pressure of norms, the menace of homophobia, and the violence of the state, but from the demands of the social. I'm all for "new and better pleasures," but I don't want to go to any meetings. (Oscar Wilde, as quoted by Phillips: "The trouble with socialism is that it takes up too many evenings.")[26] It may come across as defensive, but this disposition strikes me as utopian—not despite my disinclination to participate responsibly in social movements, but because of it.

The sexual utopianism I'm interested in doesn't aim to create a radically different world, so much as it accommodates and amplifies something we already have; heaven, it turns out, is a place on earth. Its optimism—or "queer optimism," to borrow Michael Snediker's concept—expresses "an attunement to the not yet, and a queer perspectival shift toward or refraction of an interesting present," as Shaka McGlotten writes.[27] It is as much about enjoying the pleasures of this moment as it is about pursuing new and better pleasures; the former inspires the latter, fueled by a healthy appetite for pleasure, a nose for abundance, an abiding interest in the new, and an ability to tolerate or enjoy risk. When I cruise, I not only hope to find someone desirable, I anticipate that there will always be another desirable person around the corner; this allows me to keep things loose, to move on, and to keep moving, even as I enjoy myself along the way. When I part ways after sex, I imagine that what lies ahead might not only be different, but also pleasurable, perhaps in unforeseen ways. The thing is, it can be hard to know whether my prospects in the future are good or bad. When I leave someone of my own accord, I hope that my prospects will be as good as, if not better than, what I have in the present. In this way, sexual utopianism prioritizes self-gratification, creating a paradoxical culture of detachment, of perpetually moving on to the next best thing. Needless to say, one person's sociable utopia is another's neoliberal hell. What a shame it would be—for the market, and those of us in it—if cruisers were to abandon bathhouses and rest areas because we didn't want to be bad neoliberals with maladjusted egos. On this score, it might be helpful to remember that, as Tom Roach argues (citing Foucault), "dating and hookup apps may exacerbate *homo economicus*'s ruthlessness," but they also "create a context in which a destructive ego might be humbled. More radically, they create a context in which egos and 'selves' are frequently beside the point."[28]

Open relationships and polyamory may be having a moment, but heteronorms still place a premium on monogamy.[29] Adult relationships are supposed to be with one person at a time and they're supposed to last; when they don't, they're often seen as failing rather than simply ending. But what if we thought about relationships in the way we think about sex? The fact that most of us have sex repeatedly in life—including monogamously—rather than just once or twice doesn't mean that sex fails; a single orgasm isn't meant to be permanently satiating. Part of the pleasure of sex is in the process and cycle of it, in finishing and starting again. As Gila Ashtor writes, an " 'enlarged' sexuality" is not oriented toward discharge so much as it expresses "a specific tendency towards the increase of tension and the pursuit of excitation."[30] When a relationship ends or opens up, it makes possible that moment when desire lands on a new object and begins its transformation into pleasure. This isn't just about sex or relationships, it's a general sensibility characterized by the conviction that there are always worthwhile experiences around the corner. This conviction need not stem from dissatisfaction or frustration, but can also emerge from the repeated experience of abundant and unforeseen pleasures.

7

Plaything

What are you looking for? Your options on Grindr are "chat," "dates," "friends," "networking," "relationship," and the true purpose of the app, as many would have it: "hookups."[1]

I'm not sure what exactly I was looking for when Jeremy and I first started messaging. His profile was brief, like my own. It said that he was bi and discreet—suspicious, yet hot. I know that it's biphobic to suspect that non-trans men who identify as bi just haven't come to terms with being gay yet. The desire for discretion only feeds this suspicion. But just as bi men actually exist, so do gay men who transitionally identify as bi to ease into our turpitude, as do gay men who strategically identify as bi to enhance their masculinity, since bi men are presumed to be more masculine because of their attraction to women. A bi top is less suspicious than a bi bottom since topping is thought to be the sine qua non of masculinity. The fantasy is that a man, mostly straight, might be just so horny, so voracious and insatiable that he's willing to top another man. Maybe his girlfriend or, even better, wife doesn't like anal or giving head. This might also be part of the fantasy; that the gay man who seduces a straight guy is competing with (and besting) non-trans women who are unwilling or unable to do what he will, or who can't do it as skillfully.

Jeremy's profile had no photo, but he sent one when I asked. He was young, white, husky, and hairy—a "cub." I found him attractive in a regular Joe kind of way; he was neither too polished nor too rough. Usually I'm a little apprehensive about committing to sex before meeting someone first (not that it stops me), but there was no question in my mind that I wanted Jeremy. I felt the excitement of having hooked a fish, and I was nervous about whether I would be able to reel it in.

We messaged sporadically for a month, which is usually a bad sign. I didn't want to come on too strong, but I worried that things would fizzle if there wasn't any forward movement, so I finally offered to host. He deferred: he was in the process of moving to a new place and it was taking up all his time. A few weeks later I offered again, and again he deferred—he was badly sunburned, he said—through he insisted that he really did want to get together. Shortly thereafter we finally scheduled a date and he didn't back out.

In person, Jeremy didn't look exactly like his photos, but I was still undeniably attracted to him. It wasn't just his face and body, but also his presence. His demeanor was masculine, but not aggressive or arrogant. He was friendly, responsive, polite, and playful, but also a little shy. I offered him a beer, which he accepted. I sat on the sofa, and he sat across from me in an armchair. We made small talk while the summer Olympics played in the background. He was neither standoffish nor flirtatious. I told him that he could join me on the sofa if he wanted. Side by side, we watched a few more minutes of women's volleyball before I kissed him.

My father is a cinephile who reliably dislikes romantic comedies. He complains about the lack of depth; why do these insipid characters even like each other? Romantic relationships—at least the meaningful ones—are supposed to be rooted in an appreciation of the other person's specific personality, history, perspective, and interior life, which provides a foundation for mutual understanding, respect, and care. Relationships might begin on the surface, in finding someone physically attractive, in being drawn to their presence, but are ultimately sustained by developing intimacy.

My desire for Jeremy had nothing to do with knowing or understanding him, and everything to do with his appearance and our superficial interactions. I was attracted to and envious of the masculine way he looked, carried himself, and spoke, and our sexual chemistry was strong. Knowing hardly anything about him allowed me to imagine him as I wanted. Guys like him didn't cross my path often, and I wanted to keep meeting up with him, especially at first when everything was still new and tenuous.

After a few months, a routine emerged: how often we'd meet, the order of events, how long the whole thing would take. Our sex dates had a kind of utilitarian feeling, with a side of chitchat, like getting a haircut. He had a roommate, so we only ever met at my apartment. This routine set me at ease, though I started to worry that he'd grow bored, which is how I'd felt about many of my Grindr hookups after we'd met a few times. I also worried that he might start to date a woman monogamously. (He told me that he wanted to sleep with men, but not date them, which was fine with me; I already had a boyfriend back in New York and wasn't looking for another.) I wondered whether he had informally dedicated this period of his life to having sex with men, so that when his family started to pressure him to get married and have kids, he'd feel sated enough to move on to monogamous heterosexuality. After that maybe he'd come over once a year, full of shame and lust, or we'd take fishing trips with empty tackle boxes, like Jack and Ennis in *Brokeback Mountain*.

I didn't want Jeremy's attraction to me to dissipate before my attraction to him did. It was a problem that I found him so hot, that our sex worked so well, and that I hadn't found anyone else who could compare. I auditioned guys to replace him and was usually disappointed, even when the sex was okay. Some guys were too talkative, bossy, or needy. Others were bad kissers, unhygienic, or too submissive. Each of these guys seemed to confirm the chemistry I had with Jeremy. I wondered if he had other options, or if I was competing mainly with the prowess and convenience of his own hand.

I figured that if I could seduce him a little, it might buy me some additional time, should I want it. I strategically offered him sporadic compliments, in case he craved positive feedback. Affirmation is meaningful in proportion to its scarcity. Why else struggle for the approval of those who repeatedly demonstrate that they're difficult to please? Why else be willfully difficult to please if not to wield power over those who believe that the scarcity of your approval increases its value? Occasionally I made unforced errors. A little too early on, I told him that I liked seeing him—a vague compliment that required little in the way of courage. I was trying to coax some reassurance out of him. But I said it too quietly, and had to repeat myself, failing to reproduce the sincere but casual tone I had carefully affected the first time around. "Me too," he replied, but it sounded like a question—"Me too?"—as if he were wondering where I was going with this.

The things about me that had intrigued other guys didn't seem to register with Jeremy. He wasn't charmed by my intellect, wit, or taste. Nor did he appear impressed that I was a professor, that I was in a band, or that I was handy. He seemed neither smitten with me nor aloof. He was pleasant, neutral, the kind of person who is easy to talk to at a party, but about whom you learn little in the process. This only increased my resolve to gain the upper hand. And when I discovered that it would not be easy, I began to enjoy the effort.

Cruising tends to be anonymous, transactional, and brief. When the sex is over, you part ways, and that is usually that. This places a limit on the games that can be played. A struggle for power barely begins before you're pulling your pants back up and saying toodeloo.[2]

And yet, a random weeknight Grindr hookup sometimes turns into something more: a friend, boyfriend, fuck buddy, husband, acquaintance, or contact. These relationships can be fleeting or enduring; sexual, amorous, or platonic; uncomplicated or fraught; consistent or unpredictable. As queer theorist Michael Warner writes, "Between tricks and lovers and exes and friends and fuckbuddies and bar friends' tricks and tricks' bar friends and gal pals and companions 'in the life,' queers have an astonishing range of intimacies"—or what we might simply call relations. He continues, "The impoverished vocabulary of straight culture tells us that people should either be husbands and wives or (nonsexual) friends." Writing in 1999, Warner recognized that this was already beginning to change under the influence of queer culture. Indeed, the past decade has seen a decline in the rate of marriage and an expansion of alternative relationship types, from "situationships" to friends with benefits to polyamory to open relationships. The menu of ways to be together sexually and romantically is a lot longer than it once was, even as monogamy remains the norm.

Alternative relationship styles tend to be normatively palatable to the extent that they can be framed as aligned with dominant values. For example, polyamory might be acceptable if it's about fostering compassion (or "compersion"), honesty, communication, and intimacy. An open relationship might be tolerable if it's "only sex" and therefore not a threat to one's primary relationship. And friends with benefits could be a way to enjoy sex and companionship—and ease loneliness—while waiting for that special someone to come along. But there is one relationship style that resists normative reframing: let's call it "playing games," or more specifically "playing hard to get." The dynamic that animates this relationship style is antagonistic and competitive. In its purest form, both people strategically vacillate between flirtatious expressions of interest and disinterest to extract what they want from the other person. This can continue and extend the playful flirting that sometimes precedes sex in cruising. For those of us who enjoy playing longer games with our objects of desire, the problem with cruising is only that it's too short.

Playing hard to get is often associated with the gendered power struggle of stereotypical heterosexual courtship: men want sex and a challenge, while women want commitment. For women, playing hard to get functions as a strategy to maintain men's interest until an ironclad commitment from them can be secured. For men, it functions as a way to manipulate women into sex without conceding any real commitment. A whole industry exists to guide women—or maybe just the "basic," white, non-trans ones—through this quagmire, with its ambiguities, confusions, disappointments, and agonies. Consider, for example, the following lengthy piece of advice on how long women should wait before responding to a text message from a man, taken from the popular self-help book *Not Your Mother's Rules*:

> Our official answer about when to respond to a first text is to wait somewhere between four and twenty-four hours, depending on your age. Four hours is for the younger set—for those in college and women in their early to mid-twenties who grew up with texting and Facebook. The older you are, the longer you should try to wait. For example, a thirty-year-old should wait more like twelve hours, and a forty-plus-year-old should wait a day to reply.
>
> But it's a little more complicated than that. If a guy texts you for the first time at, say, 9 or 10 a.m., you wouldn't write back exactly four hours later while you're at school or work because, theoretically, you are not checking your phone all day long. You would wait until after you clock out and leave, whenever that is. If our suggested minimum wait time falls during the middle of your day, keep waiting! Remember that it is a minimum and you can't be expected to look at your phone all the time—or give the impression that you do.
>
> If a guy texts you for the first time in the late afternoon, say at 3 or 4 p.m., you should write back later in the evening, after the time you would be at happy hour or dinner with friends. You can even wait until the next morning—what if you got home late from a movie? In this case, you're giving the impression that you're out doing something fun in the evenings rather than sitting around and fiddling with your phone.

If a guy first texts you after 8 p.m., you should not write back four hours later at midnight, even if you are in the younger age group. You're better off waiting until the next day to avoid late-night texting. In this case, you should write back on your way to class or work the next morning.

These text-back times do not apply to weekends, specifically from Friday at 6 p.m. to Sunday at 6 p.m.; this zone is a "blackout period." Just like airlines have blackout periods in which you can't use your frequent-flier points, so do Rules Girls! Weekends are a dead zone. You're unavailable, you're unreachable, you're busy, you're gone! But don't get mad that he's texting you on Saturday. He may have been spoiled by non-Rules Girls who put up with or even initiate weekend text chatfests—but you aren't one of them! Don't text lecture him with "Why are you texting me on Saturday? Why didn't you just ask me out by Wednesday for Saturday?" Instead, silently show him that you are not available by not responding at all during the weekend so he knows he must make plans in advance in the future. You can text him back on Sunday night, "Thanks, sounded good, but I already had plans." The only exception to this Rule is if he already asked you out by Wednesday for Saturday night and is texting during the dead zone to confirm plans. Otherwise, you are blocked out from casual texting on the weekends.

There is, however, one exception to waiting: if he needs an answer right away because he wants to buy concert tickets or something else time-sensitive and needs to make sure the date is good for you, you can quickly write back, "Hey, the 14th at 8 p.m. sounds great tx!" But do not abuse this exception or use it as an opportunity to start an unnecessary longer conversation.[3]

Did you really think that if you were interested in a guy, you could text him back immediately or, even worse, initiate a text exchange?

According to prevailing heteronorms, playing hard to get with your object of desire might sometimes be a necessary evil—particularly for women who want to tame men—but is generally considered bad behavior. Well-adjusted adults aren't supposed to play in relationships ("don't play with me," "you got played"), instead they're supposed to be real, authentic, honest, communicative, and forthright. The phrase "playing games" evokes the immaturity of youth and the unseriousness of play.[4] When we play hard to get, we try to manipulate someone else to get something from them that we suspect they wouldn't give us otherwise: desire, affection, time and attention, sex, commitment, money, gifts. In the passage above, this is done by withdrawing attention and feigning being busy and popular, which produces an overall impression of not liking a guy too much; once it seems like you like a guy too much, it's all over—he's got all the leverage.

Playing hard to get is more normatively palatable when the goal is love—or rather, securing a boyfriend/girlfriend, partner, or spouse—and less palatable when we have no interest in commitment, when the other person is just a plaything.[5] Withholding sex until the other person commits to you is more acceptable than withholding affirmation to extract sex. It is for this reason that *The Game*, journalist Neill Strauss's ethnographic investigation of male pickup artists (which doubles as a guide to manipulating women), received a chilly critical reception, despite its commercial success.[6] Treating other people like your plaything is generally seen as immature, unkind, and irresponsible, if not unethical, and "players" are thought to be damaged somehow: selfish, unable to feel empathy, give (or accept) love, and grow up. In a word: sociopathic.

Things get more interesting when the goal of playing games is not to get something from someone—as often seems the case in a heterosexual context, at least in theory—but rather to experience the pleasure of struggling for power; when the game is not a means to an end but an end in and of itself. This is how Evangelos Tziallas understands Grindr: not primarily as a tool to find sex, but rather a game that entails "participatory surveillance" and "self-pornification."[7] Unlike work, which most of us do primarily for the money, play is characteristically its own end, as Georg Simmel pointed out long ago.[8] In contrast to work, play promises pleasure in the present; this is its primary purpose, and also what makes it so appealing and useful to the psyche. For some of us, there is a lot of pleasure in playing with others, and in being played with, especially when this involves suspending work, reality, or whatever the opposite of play is. What a drag relationships can be, especially when they become work, and when we're supposed to work on them.[9] Why not just play instead, indefinitely? Writing about the Eliot Spitzer scandal (and the scandal of sex in general), Lauren Berlant asks, "Who knows what sex could be if people were encouraged to enjoy it as play rather than as a drama?"[10]

If this seems like clever branding—"play" sounds better than "manipulate"—it might be because norms make it difficult to entertain the notion that struggling for power with our objects of desire, trying to gain leverage over them as they do the same to us, can be fun or even thrilling.

How might I turn the tables in my favor? Getting too personal with Jeremy could freak him out, or compromise my attraction to him, but I thought that if I knew just a little more about him, I might be able to better sculpt my presentation of self in the shape of his desire and thereby gain some leverage. Between rounds of sex, I asked general questions about his family, friends, and past relationships; his taste—music, television, movies, humor; and his job, hobbies, and politics. He answered my questions without revealing much, and rarely reciprocated my curiosity. Game on.

The less he said, the less nervous I felt about asking. Could I really not pull something useful out of him? I asked him if he was the kind of person who solicits other people for advice. Was he vengeful? Was he jealous? *No, no,* and *no, but I am competitive.* (Useful!) I asked him about his dating prospects as if this represented no threat to our continued sex, and he said that it wasn't easy to meet someone smart. Whatever he meant by this, I took it as a compliment. I asked him if he thought that his best friend—a hetero woman—was in love with him. *No.* I asked him if he talked to his friends about their dating and sex lives. *Not really.*

Phillips understands this kind of knowledge gathering in relationships as a psychic strategy to manage our dependence on others and thereby prevent or lessen the pain we'll feel if they leave us or are unable or unwilling to satisfy our desires. To put it more simply, we want to know other people so that we can control them and protect ourselves from disappointment and rejection.[11] Of course, this doesn't really work. No matter how hard we try to know and control others, we can still be abandoned by them. And no matter how well we believe we know ourselves, we can never be certain about what we really want or who we might become in the future. It is for this reason that Phillips advocates for psychoanalysis not as a tool of self-knowledge, but rather as a "treatment that weans people from their compulsion to understand and be understood . . . ," which is essentially a compulsion to control the uncontrollable.[12] As liberating as this sounds, I'm not sure I want to give up the pleasure that this compulsion can yield when a certain balance is struck between one person's aggression and another's resistance.

Was Jeremy playing hard to get? Had he seen through my apparently innocent curiosity? Could he sense that my inquiries were strategic? Was his nonchalance equally calculated? Or was he taciturn by nature, a private person—maybe just with the guys he was fucking (because, like he said, he wanted only sex)? I wasn't sure, which was unsettling but also fun. In the end it doesn't matter what was going on for him; whatever the case, I enjoyed him as a worthy opponent.

I wanted a way to make him jealous, to inflame his desire, not that it had yet waned. What a marvel of the psyche that a jilted lover can become sexy again simply by seeming less available to us than they once were, and maybe especially when they've got someone new and attractive in their bed. I'd had plenty of sex with other people since Jeremy and I first met, but I couldn't find a way to use that to my advantage without risking turning him off.

For a while we took turns soliciting dates. Were we both keeping score, or was that just me? When it was my turn to reach out, I'd occasionally delay, not because I was trying to train him to respect me (as suggested in *Not Your Mother's Rules*), but because I felt desired when he initiated communication, and I wanted to see if his desire was stronger than his pride. Usually it wasn't, but in another week or two he'd relent if I didn't first. Our routine long since established, he'd nevertheless ask me what my week looked like. I'd suggest the same day and time as always and he'd reply, "That might work."

As a child, I learned that men are supposed to pursue women, and not the other way around. Maybe this has changed; I really wouldn't know. This clarification of roles—who is supposed to chase, who is supposed to be chased—would have spoiled the game for me; another reason I love being gay. The pleasure of Jeremy's reappearance was heightened by the fact that I could just as easily have contacted him (in the absence of gendered norms); it was a staring contest. This pleasure faded during periods when I became less available, and Jeremy would solicit me repeatedly. "I'll definitely let you know when I'm free next," I'd reassure him, and yet he'd still continue to reach out. I wasn't playing hard to get, I was just busy, though the effect was the same. He didn't seem upset by this—he'd always say "no worries" when I told him I was unavailable—though he'd also occasionally mention that he missed meeting more regularly. I should have found this gratifying as evidence of the durability of his interest in having sex with me, but the more time that passed, the less I was concerned about this. During these periods, I began to miss his resistance; I missed feeling like his plaything. I still enjoyed having sex with him, but some of the charge was gone.

My relationship with Jeremy felt most exciting when I was neither too nervous that he would end things nor too certain that he wouldn't. It was the possibility of his departure that made his presence feel meaningful. You might think I wouldn't want to worry about this, but my pleasure depended on it; I enjoyed that he chose not to withdraw, over and over. If wedlock quells some people's anxiety about being abandoned (by making it legally, socially, and financially harder to leave), it can also extinguish the pleasure of feeling desired. I imagine that this is why some people want to put a ring on it—they can't tolerate the possibility that their partner's desire is fickle—despite the damage a ring can do to their own desirability.

Freudian psychoanalysis proposes that power is not an addition to our sexuality—as if we could be rid of it, arriving at some kind of purely egalitarian sexuality—but rather is its primary content.[13] We can't eliminate power from sex, but we might be able to negotiate it in ways that maximize our pleasure. Playing hard to get with our objects of desire—our playthings—can be one way to do this.

We typically think of desire as the beginning of a psychic process that culminates in pleasure (or its frustration), but there can also be pleasure in desiring, in wanting someone or something, whether or not the wanted person or thing is ultimately acquired. Less obviously, wanting someone can feel good because of their distance. If satisfying one's desire can be pleasurable, so too can delaying one's satisfaction. As Jesper Juul points out in *The Art of Failure*, games that are too easy to win are not fun to play, and neither are games that are impossible to win.[14] When I toy with my playthings, and am toyed with by them, I want not only to win, but also to be pleasurably agitated. These goals are in tension because winning, satisfying though it may be, ends the pleasure of playing. I wanted to have power over Jeremy, but I also took pleasure in his resistance, as frustrating as it could be.

This pleasurable aspect of frustration, or frustrating aspect of pleasure, can be intensified by getting involved with people who are skilled at playing hard to get. A relationship with someone who balances withholding with surrendering can be pleasurably excruciating, like being edged during sex. It's not simply that those of us who enjoy this kind of thing are willing to tolerate a lover's distance in pursuit of pleasure, but that we require it. This is part of the appeal of a particular kind of masculinity to me, especially in terms of emotions; whatever a masculine person may be feeling or not feeling, they're probably not going to tell me. And the less I know, the less I can control, though I will enjoy trying.

In a passage from *Beyond the Pleasure Principle*, Freud observes his toddler grandson playing a kind of peek-a-boo game, which Freud calls "fort-da" (gone-there), in which the child throws a wooden reel out of sight and then pulls it back with an attached string. Freud understands this game as the child's attempt to cope with his mother's occasional absence: the pleasure that accompanies the reappearance of the wooden reel compensates the child for the pain of the loss of his mother. Freud writes, "Her departure had to be enacted as necessary preliminary to her joyful return . . ."[15] Maybe there is no pleasure without misfortune: the internalized phallic male (Bersani), the absent mother (Freud). In a world often indifferent to our desires—for some of us more than others, probably—it might not be such a terrible thing to learn to bear frustration or, even better, to take pleasure in it, conservative as this may sound. Phillips argues that our fantasies of satisfaction can be dangerous when motivated by a desire for revenge. But these fantasies can also sustain the pleasure of desiring, which can be an end in and of itself, as Tiana Reid observes.[16]

Citing Freud, Stanley Fish writes: "For the masochist, 'it is the suffering itself that matters; whether the sentence is cast by a loved one or by an indifferent person is of no importance; it may even be caused by impersonal forces or circumstances, but the true masochist always holds out his cheek whenever he sees a chance of receiving a blow.'"[17] And so I imagined it might be with Jeremy, whose interest in our sex never wavered, but in whose behavior I could nevertheless identify signs of ambivalence. When your pleasure depends on these signs, you become an expert at identifying them; even the most adoring lover sometimes focuses their attention elsewhere. Maybe I'm a masochist in this regard. Then again, Bersani argues that sexuality itself is a tautology for masochism; there's no escaping it.[18]

One good thing about a lover who enjoys ambivalence is that they are, by necessity, undemanding, relatively speaking. They might be aggressive—as I could be—but push too far and the game will end one way or another. This makes possible a kind of freedom that is motivated by pleasure rather than ethics. Whether I'm the aggressor or the target of aggression, I like the idea that aggression can be kept in check by self-interest rather than fellow-feeling. For one, it seems like a better sell. Additionally, it assumes interpersonal antagonism rather than alignment, the latter of which is a tall order and an imposition. That's how I prefer my aggression: directed at those best able to resist—not because it's more ethical, but because it's more pleasurable—and coming from those I can easily leave behind should I so desire.

Just as I enjoyed Jeremy's resistance, I imagine that my aggression might have been part of his pleasure—the pleasure of feeling desired and of having temporary leverage over another person. Every time I displayed interest in him, I produced an opportunity for him to exercise the power to withhold or refuse. You can't meaningfully refuse something that hasn't been offered. But my offer was also contingent on, even calibrated to, his resistance. I didn't want to be intimate with him so much as I wanted him to resist my efforts at intimacy: an arm-wrestling contest without end. I always thought that Jeremy was hotter than most of the other guys I'd hooked up with, but maybe he was just a particularly well-matched competitor.

There is nothing particularly surprising about the pleasure of satisfied aggression. When an athlete scores a point in a challenging game or match, of course they yell and pump their fist in the air. The pleasure of powerlessness is more surprising, as Bersani argues. Writing about BDSM, Bersani proposes that its most radical function "is not primarily in exposing the hypocritically denied centrality of erotically stimulating power plays in 'normal' society; it lies rather in the shocking revelation that, for the sake of that stimulation, humans may be willing to give up control over their environment."[19] The reversibility of roles in BDSM is interesting to Bersani not because it reveals these roles to be constructed rather than natural (as some defenders of BDSM have argued), but because it suggests that the pleasure of domination is linked to the pleasure of submission, of renouncing control. More strongly stated, it is possible that domination only produces pleasure insofar as it shadowed by an impulse to self-shatter.

I like this idea, maybe because I enjoy imagining that masculinity is an elaborate ruse to intensify the disavowed pleasure of submission. What can I say, I like masc guys who love to bottom, even the bossier, less submissive ones. But Bersani's linking of domination with submission also resonates more broadly with what I have described here as the pleasure of playing hard to get: of resisting, then submitting, then resisting again, then submitting again. However nonchalant and casual Jeremy could be, our sex always felt like a kind of submission, an acknowledgment (however fleeting) of the intensity of his desire, though he didn't seem particularly submissive to me while bottoming, even with his legs high in the air, instructing me to fuck him forcefully and then whimpering when I did.

This is not to defend playing hard to get against those who find it immature, narcissistic, unhealthy, or pathological. As with the other desires and pleasures I've explored here, I'm more curious about how the game works and what it can set into motion than I am interested in justifying its existence according to the dictates of ethics, politics, or psychology. In all likelihood, it will be nobody's salvation or downfall. It's just one way to hold our dominant and submissive tendencies in a kind of pleasurable tension, if we can bear the frustration of stiff competition.

As a reader, too, I enjoy a balance between being pushed by an author and pushing back, between being seduced and being skeptical. If all books begin with an author cruising a reader, once things get going, reading is less like sex than like the flirtatious games that can follow it, as an author tries to tell a story, set up a question, offer a theory, articulate or challenge a truth, reveal an ambiguity, think a new thought, and play around with language. A reader either finds it engaging or they don't. The best readers, in my opinion, are promiscuous: they carry around with them the imprint of all the authors with whom they've flirted, and they're committed to none of them, ultimately. This isn't a value judgment, I just mean that choices tend to be meaningful in proportion to the number of options from which they're selected, and that sleeping around can be a good way to learn some things and forget others.

When I read, I generally want things to be orderly: coherent, consistent, methodical, and intelligible. But sex is not about order. Or maybe it is for some people, when they desire what they're supposed to desire, and they feel what they're supposed to feel, and there is no allure to transgression, no excitation too disturbing, unsettling, or shattering, and no surprising pleasure that forces a reconsideration of who they believe themselves to be. For the rest of us, sex is often disordering, which is a good reason to be suspicious of scholars who write about sex. To quote Phillips's insight once again: "In giving an account we make of sexuality, of our desire, something that it is not and can never be. It is as though we are trying to stop it having its effect, prevent it taking its course."[20] Sex doesn't need to be anything other than what it is—whatever that may be—but perhaps it holds a lesson for reading and writing alike, especially writing about sex, which is that the satisfaction of order is ultimately no match for the pleasures of disorder.

Sex is also not about being good, try as we might to bring our desires into alignment with our values, beliefs, ideology, faith, or sense of self, if and when there's a mismatch. This is another good reason to be suspicious of scholars who defend our perversions by establishing their harmlessness or utility. Defense is an understandable political response to pathologization, as is anger or rage. The problem is that defense stifles thought in the process. The limiting of our curiosity—our ability to observe, question, speculate, and imagine—is a missed opportunity not just to think *about* sex, but to think more *like* sex: allowing our appetite for pleasure to displace, if only temporarily, our focus on who's coming after us, and whether or not we're good people. This might be another lesson that sex offers to thought: sometimes pleasure is more important to us than being safe or being good.

I can't deny that I'm drawn to the objects of each chapter—impersonality, fetishization, masculinity, rejection, fungibility, and game playing—not only because of their role in my sex life, but because of the ways they've been pathologized by conservatives and liberals alike. Neither can I deny that I still feel the impulse to defend myself. It's a political instinct that I try to quiet so that I can become curious again. There is a popular saying (falsely attributed to Oscar Wilde; the actual source is unknown): "Everything is about sex, except sex, which is about power." But how to think about sex and power—and identity, otherness, sociality, and so on—without subjecting sex to judgment or requiring it to serve a higher purpose, especially when you've got Marx in one ear and Freud in the other? Perhaps this is "a paradox to manage, not a problem to solve," as Esther Perel remarks of a similar paradox: our simultaneous desires for security and adventure.[21]

It can be frustrating to be pulled in multiple directions without resolution, but it can also be fun, if that's something you're into. I'm reminded again of Gila Ashtor's argument that an enlarged sexuality is not about "discharge" but rather increasing tension and pursuing excitation.[22] In this case, climax—conclusion—is not something to be pursued, but rather staved off as we find out how well we're able to tolerate the pleasures of friction and uncertainty. It's possible that the ways we relate to each other and to our own "constitutive antagonisms"[23] will be changed in the process. But honestly, it just feels good.

Notes

Prologue

1. River Page [@river_is_nice].
2. Page, "Don't Be a Bigot, It's 'Houseless' Now."
3. Cruising is hardly exclusive to US gay culture—and is also practiced by men who don't identify as gay—but the "emic knowledge" that grounds this book is from the position of a US citizen and resident, and more specifically a Northeasterner and New Yorker.
4. Gay slang for men with few sexual limits.
5. For my purposes here, the contemporary left in the US is united by a shared ethical commitment to caring for others seen as socially disadvantaged, marginalized, oppressed, and/or exploited. As part of this commitment, the left now generally supports—or at least gives lip service to—the civil rights and social inclusion of sexual minorities, while the right tends to be less accepting. For example, in 2020 the Pew Research Center reported that 86 percent of left-identified people in the US believe that "homosexuality should be accepted by society" versus 53 percent of the right. That said, a more nuanced political typology is sometimes necessary to describe variation within the left and right, and to accommodate the many Americans whose views are not uniformly left or right. The Pew Center's latest political typology identifies nine salient political subgroups in the US and finds significant differences between the "progressive left" and "establishment liberals," as well as between "democratic mainstays" and the "outside left"—though all four left subgroups are primarily aligned with the Democratic Party. When considering different left responses to sexual non-normativity, I find it useful to distinguish between "liberals" (which groups together the more centrist "establishment liberals" and "democratic mainstays") and "progressives" (which groups together the less centrist "progressive left" and "outside left"). Additional categories and descriptors are sometimes necessary for greater analytical precision, for example, the queer and feminist left, the radical left. While conservative responses to sexual non-normativity also vary, I am less

concerned here with the right, hence my use of the monolithic "conservative." That said, it may be the case that conservatives are sometimes more tolerant of some of the desires and behaviors I examine here—for example, the exalting of masculinity, albeit by men who have sex with men (MSM)—than are critics on the left. See Poushter and Kent, "The Global Divide on Homosexuality Persists"; "Beyond Red vs. Blue."

    6. Hardy and Easton, *The Ethical Slut, Third Edition*.

    7. For the moment, I'm ignoring my familial communism and paternal Semitism.

    8. Yet I'm tickled by John Waters: "I had more fun when it was illegal to be gay." Smith, "John Waters on the Mainstreaming of Gay Culture."

    9. *One-Dimensional Queer*.

    10. See Amin, "We Are All Nonbinary."

    11. Warner, "Queer and Then?"

    12. See also Edelman, *Bad Education*, 20.

    13. "Queer Texts, Bad Habits, and the Issue of a Future," 249.

    14. Kerri, "The Lowest Form of Humor."

    15. Espinoza, *Cruising*, 197.

    16. Phillips, *Missing Out*, 79.

    17. "Thinking with Pleasure," 145.

    18. Corey and Nakayama, "Sextext." As quoted in Huff, "On [Be]Coming in Boystown," 431.

    19. This focus on intersectionality initially emerged as a corrective to queer theory's whiteness. As Amber Jamilla Musser succinctly summarizes Chandan Reddy's critique: "Sexuality as a frame silences race." But as Dean and Davis argue (citing Robyn Wiegman), intersectionality's juridical imagination does not transfer well to theory, leading to a "queer-superhero-in-tights syndrome." Musser, *Sensational Flesh*, 18; Davis and Dean, *Hatred of Sex*, 58; Wiegman, *Object Lessons*.

    20. If sex and sexuality are fundamentally messy, and messiness is a queer condition, as Martin F. Manalansan IV has argued, then we might conclude that, in at least this sense, all sex is queer. Manalansan, "The 'Stuff' of Archives."

    21. As Bersani writes, "De-gaying gayness can only fortify homophobic oppression; it accomplishes in its own way the principal aim of homophobia: the elimination of gays." *Homos*, 5. It is not just my curiosity, but also my indignation that keeps me on task when I imagine having to talk about this book with people in my life who may find it somewhat inappropriate, embarrassing, or otherwise unpleasant.

    22. *Underdogs*, 142.

    23. I was a student of Patricia Clough, who wrote *The End(s) of Ethnography*.

    24. *Underdogs*, 136.

    25. "Like," 88.

    26. *Monogamy*, 101.

Chapter 1

1. Freud, "On the Universal Tendency to Debasement in the Sphere of Love," 189.
2. Edelman, "Men's Room." See also Goldberg, "Lust Room."
3. Hunt et al., "Changes in Condom Use by Gay Men."
4. Califia, *Public Sex*, 65.
5. Habib, "Rest Stop Confidential."
6. Pathologization can also be an internal affair, as cruisers themselves sometimes see cruising as a flaw, fault, or failure. See McGlotten, *Virtual Intimacies*.
7. Rubin, "Thinking Sex."
8. Rubin, 111.
9. Delany, *Times Square Red, Times Square Blue*.
10. Jamie Hakim offers a similar defense of chemsex (that is, using drugs like meth or GHB to enhance sex) when he argues that it be understood as "a way for some, largely migrant, gay and bisexual men to experience a sense of collectivity not only in a city where the collective physical spaces they have historically gathered are closing down due to neoliberal approaches to town planning but also in a wider culture in which neoliberalism has been hegemonic and that in multiple ways alienates them from experiencing the possibility of collectivity at all." *Work That Body*, 112.
11. To take another recent example, Adeyemi, Khubchandani, and Rivera-Servera argue that we need queer nightlife "because it archives politics (elsewhere undocumented) through gesture, memory, DJing techniques, promotional fliers, architecture." "Introduction," 10.
12. "Introduction," 1.
13. For more on this confusion, see Davis and Dean, *Hatred of Sex*, 58.
14. For similar reasons, I am unwilling to embrace defense as the most ethical course of action—if indeed it is—in proportion to my privilege. There are more important things to me here than being good.
15. Foucault, *Foucault Live: Collected Interviews, 1961–1984*, 382. Richardson provides another example of this kind of thinking: "When my nameless friend and I have sex in public we liberate ourselves from oppressive heteronormative conceptions of sexual identity and respectable sexual behavior (order) and ride the edge of sexual ambiguity and disreputable sexual behaviors (chaos) by transforming a nonsexual everyday space into a sexual space for exploring queered pleasure." "Queering Edgework."
16. See, for example, Nguyen, *A View from the Bottom*; Hart, *Between the Body and the Flesh*; Tuhkanen, "Rigorously Speculating: An Interview with Leo Bersani."
17. *Screen Love*, 22.
18. Richardson, "Constructing Lesbian Sexualities," 282; "To Suffer Pleasure," 254.

19. *No Future*, 17, 29.
20. 29.
21. 30, 31.
22. See, for example: Adorno, "On the Fetish Character in Music and the Regression of Listening"; Adorno and Simpson, "On Popular Music."
23. "The Use of Pleasure in Harm Reduction," 420.
24. Delany, *Times Square Red, Times Square Blue*, 185.
25. As part of this effort, good kinds of pleasure are sometimes distinguished from bad kinds. As Tim Dean argues, "False pleasure—perhaps an unexamined cognate of false consciousness—is pleasure that can be demystified as gratification obtained at our expense, whether by the dominant gender, the ruling class, or the hegemonic economic system." Dean, "The Biopolitics of Pleasure," 482. For more on pro-social pleasure, see Fine and Corte, "Group Pleasures," in which the authors distinguish pleasure (as an individual pursuit) from fun (as social). For examples of the valuing of collaborative pleasures, see Goldberg, *Antisocial Media*, 58.
26. For example, there is a long-standing fantasy among Marxist scholars that a systemic reorganization of labor from being competitive and privately owned to being cooperative and publicly organized will resolve alienation, making it newly possible for the proletariat to enjoy sacrificing their time and energy for the collective good. See Goldberg, *Antisocial Media*, 136–38.
27. Lorde, *A Burst of Light*, 139; Parker-Pope, "Why Self-Care Isn't Selfish."
28. Dean, "Uses of Perversity," 169.
29. As David M. Halperin notes, these forms of disapproval are often framed and justified in relation to alleged danger and harm. "Introduction," 4.
30. *Hatred of Sex*, 38.
31. One notable exception is Kane Race, who critiques the reification of "sex and drug practices as heroic acts of resistance to hegemonic orders on account of their deviant or illicit status and their transgression of social norms." Race notes that such arguments tend to "disregard multiplicity of meanings and purposes such activities may have in practice when situated in the diverse contexts of their enactment." Hakim and Race, "The Gay Scientist," 578.
32. In the wake of #MeToo there has been a renewed focus on consent in sex discourse in the US. Responding to this, Joe Fischel argues that affirmative consent is the least-bad legal standard for sexual assault law, but he also proposes that there are more important considerations for sexual justice politics, particularly in terms of building "a safer, more democratically hedonic culture." *Screw Consent*, 4. While I'm sympathetic to Fischel's interest in sexual autonomy and access, he frames these issues as a matter of ethics that can and should be dealt with through collective social action. For reasons that will soon become clear, I prefer a less other-oriented approach. Furthermore, I suspect that the contemporary embrace of affirmative consent is motivated, in part, by a desire to resolve

the confusion and ambiguity of sex—while also ignoring queer forms of sex that aren't well suited to a model of enthusiastic consent—by turning consent into a "yes" or "no" question. See Cheves, "Consent in the Dark;" Hoppe, "Lost in the Dark—Or How I Learned to Queer Consent." As Davis and Dean write, "Sex provokes extraordinary ambivalence because it may entail consenting paradoxically to one's own violation." *Hatred of Sex*, 42.

33. Chu and Berg, "Wanting Bad Things."
34. *Detransition, Baby*, 333.
35. Marx, "Theses on Feuerbach."
36. Chu and Berg, "Wanting Bad Things."
37. For this reason, I appreciate Billy Huff's candor when he writes of his desire for Black men, "So many times I have justified it to others by explaining that my political commitments prevent me from allowing myself to eroticize white men, but in truth, there does not exist an intellectual or political reflection that can blush my cheeks and rush my blood through my body like my unconscious fantasies do." "On [Be]Coming in Boystown," 440.
38. *The Queer Art of Failure*, 153.
39. *Curiosity and Power*, 3.
40. For this reason, Gila Ashtor's characterization of Eve Sedgwick's work resonates with me: "It is precisely the tension between, on the one hand, fidelity to desire's non-'Truth' and on the other, an exploration of what desire *might* mean, that organizes Sedgwick's critical project and that she enacts in her autobiographical writing." *Homo Psyche*, 53.
41. *Invitation to Sociology*.
42. Ahmed, "Orientations: Toward a Queer Phenomenology."
43. *Virtual Intimacies*, 4.
44. For more on the various kinds of risk involved in cruising, see Richardson, "Queering Edgework." For more on the specific risks of cruising public restrooms, see Goldberg, "Lust Room."
45. Here I'm thinking of Brian A. Horton's argument that the policing of cruising can cross over into the erotic play that it seeks to control. "The Police and the Policed: Queer Crossings in a Mumbai Bathroom."
46. Perel, "The Secret to Desire in a Long-Term Relationship."

Chapter 2

1. Musto, "Gay Dance Clubs on the Wane in the Age of Grindr." Of course, there are many other reasons that gay and queer people participate in nightlife, as the essays of *Queer Nightlife* attest, especially if one looks beyond the urban "gay dance clubs" patronized primarily by white gay men.

2. Rogers, "The Pines' Summer of Discontent."

3. Sharif Mowlabocus effectively answers this question in arguing that gay male subculture "is now *both* physically and digitally manifested, and that these multiple manifestations occur simultaneously and shape one another continuously." *Gaydar Culture*, 15. Kane Race similarly suggests that the important question is not whether Grindr will render obsolete in-person cruising, but rather how it transforms sexual culture on a larger scale. Race, " 'Party and Play.' "

4. I suspect that many users would find the Grindr messaging scenario Tom Roach describes quite relatable: *Screen Love*, 73–74.

5. McGlotten, *Virtual Intimacies*, 3.

6. Holmes, O'Byrne, and Murray, "Faceless Sex."

7. Humphreys, "Tearoom Trade: Impersonal Sex in Public Places," 52.

8. In this way, my experience echoes that of McGlotten's interviewees, who appreciate how in-person cruising makes possible "the unpredictable bloom of desire." *Virtual Intimacies*, 6.

9. Nelson, *On Freedom: Four Songs of Care and Constraint*.

10. This brings to mind Gilles Deleuze and Felix Guatarri's characterization of the Body without Organs as a "connection of desires, conjunction of flows, continuum of intensities." Deleuze and Guatarri, *A Thousand Plateaus*, 161.

11. Bersani, "Is the Rectum a Grave?," 217.

12. Bersani is not the first to associate sex with self-shattering; Davis writes that in the gnostic tradition, " 'sexuality remains one of the demonic forces in human consciousness,' including (at least on occasion) 'a voluptuous yearning for the extinction of one's consciousness.' " As quoted in Murray, "Self Size and Observable Sex," 158. Furthermore, Bersani borrows from Catherine MacKinnon's characterization of the "male supremacist definition of female sexuality as lust for self-annihilation." Bersani, "Is the Rectum a Grave?," 213. Bersani is, however, rather unique in praising this quality, and not because it facilitates union with another person or because it engenders compassion—the typical reasons.

13. This is not to assert that all pleasure is self-shattering. Roland Barthes famously proposed a difference between pleasures that are self-shattering and those that are self-confirming. In "Rectum," Bersani is clearly interested in the former. See Race, "Thinking with Pleasure," 146–47.

14. As Alex Espinoza writes, "The only way one gets better at both [cruising and writing] is by returning to it, doing it over and over, again and again." *Cruising*, 12.

15. Dean, *Unlimited Intimacy*, 185.

16. Alex Espinoza: "You have to practice patience when you cruise." *Cruising*, 11.

17. For an expanded definition of intimacy, see McGlotten, *Virtual Intimacies*, 1.

18. Franzen, "Liking Is for Cowards. Go for What Hurts."

19. ALOK and Mingus, "Why Ugliness Is Vital in the Age of Social Media."

20. I take this to be one motive for the focus on intimacy in books like McGlotten's *Virtual Intimacies*, Dean's *Unlimited Intimacy*, Bersani and Phillips's *Intimacies*, and Tom Roach's *Screen Love*, even as each of these titles effectively interrogates the concept. See also Berlant, "Intimacy"; Payne, *The Promiscuity of Network Culture*.

21. *Virtual Intimacies*, 47.

22. Delany, *Times Square Red, Times Square Blue*, 40.

23. For an index of some of these texts, see Attwood, Hakim, and Winch, "Mediated Intimacies."

24. For more on the specific psychoanalytic framework that informs Bersani's understanding of sexuality, and a critique of this understanding from a competing psychoanalytic framework, see "The Genealogy of Sex: Bersani, Laplanche, and Self-Shattering Sexuality" in Ashtor, *Homo Psyche*.

25. Tim Dean argues that this suspicion projects onto strangers our discomfort with our own unconscious. Through a psychic sleight of hand, we become paranoid that strangers are a threat to us, when in fact the real threat comes from our own unconscious. See Dean, "Sameness without Identity."

26. Dean notes that the term "identity" means different things in different disciplines: "While for psychology *identity* designates a self-conscious sense of selfhood, for philosophy the term refers to a non-psychological principle of unity or indiscernibility; sociologically *identity* betokens categories of classification—for instance those of gender, race, and sexuality that variably inform an individual's psychological identity while remaining irreducible to it. I note these extremely schematic distinctions merely to observe that critiques of identitarianism often draw inconsistently on discourses of identity (for example, by using a philosophical sense of non-identity to try to undermine oppressive social identities. . . ." Dean, 27–28. If I am guilty of this kind of inconsistency by putting together psychoanalysis and sociology, I hope that it is productively so.

27. See Dean, "Homosexuality and the Problem of Otherness."

28. See Marriott, "On Racial Fetishism."

29. One notable psychoanalytic exception is sexed or gendered difference; men and women are sometimes thought to be fundamentally different, psychically speaking, for example, the Oedipus complex vs. penis envy.

30. Fanon, *Black Skin, White Masks*, 152.

31. "Queer Theories from Somewhere," 64.

32. This characterization of psychoanalysis may be unjustifiably universal, but I'm partial to it anyway—as an aspiration, if nothing else. As Gila Ashtor notes, psychoanalysis has a "notorious history of schisms and splits." *Homo Psyche*, 14. After Freud's death, psychoanalysis in the US merged with psychiatry and medicine, inspiring Foucault's critique of the discipline, and queer theorists' uneasy relationship with it. See Dean and Lane, "Homosexuality & Psychoanalysis."

33. Hakim and Race, "The Gay Scientist," 581.
34. Acocella, "This Is Your Life." When teaching psychoanalytic theories that seem particularly far-fetched, I remind students that analysts talk to patients; Acocella's claim that there is "no support from evidence" glosses over this fact.
35. *Monogamy*, 31.
36. Bersani, "Sociability and Cruising," 21.
37. Holmes, O'Byrne, and Murray, "Faceless Sex," 253.
38. Holmes, O'Byrne, and Murray, 256.
39. Holmes, O'Byrne, and Murray, 257.
40. In making this argument, Holmes, O'Byrne, and Murray reference Emmanuel Levinas, who theorizes the human face as encapsulating the strangeness of the capital-O Other. When face-to-face with strangers, will we be ethical? This an important question for Levinas, and also for Holmes, O'Byrne, and Murray, who imagine that our "nakedness, vulnerability, hunger, and destitution" might be expressed not only though our faces, but through the vulnerable body parts offered defenselessly through a glory hole.
41. Bersani, *Homos*, 128.
42. Bersani, 129.
43. Again, this is my preferred overextension and literalization of Bersani's argument. I was understandably disappointed when I read Bersani, in a later interview, state: "This does not mean . . . that *ébranlement* [self-shattering] is an empirical characteristic of our sexual lives; it means that a masochistic self-shattering was constitutive of our identities as sexual beings, that it is present, always, not primarily in our orgasms but rather in the terrifying but also exhilarating instability of human subjectivity." Dean et al., "A Conversation with Leo Bersani," 5–6.
44. Seidman, *The Social Construction of Sexuality*, 86.
45. Dean, "Uses of Perversity," 270.
46. Daniel, "All Sound Is Queer," 46.
47. Roach, *Screen Love*.
48. Bersani and Phillips, *Intimacies*, 86.
49. Bersani, "Genital Chastity," 366.
50. Menon, *Indifference to Difference*. Menon's use of this term draws from Jonathan Goldberg's characterization of Eve Sedgwick's work.
51. Caserio et al., "The Antisocial Thesis in Queer Theory," 825. I think Dean puts it best when he describes Bersani's work as moving from "the antirelational to proliferating relational possibilities." In this respect, Bersani's critics are (also) antirelational; in privileging social (that is, responsible, altruistic, intersubjective) relations, they foreclose other relational possibilities. Dean, "Sex and the Aesthetics of Existence," 391.
52. In his response to this critique, Lee Edelman identifies complementary arguments—in terms of theorizing the impossibility of inhabiting an identity founded on negation—in the work of feminist and Black scholars, including Luce

Irigaray, Julia Kristeva, Catherine Malibou, Frantz Fanon, Sylvia Wynter, Jared Sexton, and Fred Moten. The queer, in Edelman's framework, is not an inhabitable sexual identity, but an irrecuperable, structural negativity that characterizes multiple forms of exclusion, including those by gender and race. *Bad Education*. Davis and Dean similarly identify a group of queer scholars who engage race while also—like Bersani—embracing "erotic debasement": Kathryn Bond Stockton, Darieck Scott, Nguyen Tan Hoang, Mary C. Foltz, and Avgi Saketopoulou. *Hatred of Sex*, 72.

53. "Punks, Bulldaggers, and Welfare Queens," 450. See also Johnson, "'Quare' Studies, or (Almost) Everything I Know about Queer Studies I Learned from My Grandmother."

54. Again, Bersani's answer to this question is that identification/differentiation motivates this violence in the first place.

55. "'Quare' Studies, or (Almost) Everything I Know about Queer Studies I Learned from My Grandmother."

56. Menon describes the task of her book on queer universalism as rethinking "the line of predictability that gets drawn from the body to identity, and from desire to the self." *Indifference to Difference*, 1.

57. *Bad Education*, 20.

58. Edelman, 31.

59. For further critique of Muñoz, see Goldberg, *Antisocial Media*, 29–30.

60. *Hatred of Sex*, 77.

61. Morris, "My Mustache, My Self."

62. For an extended rumination on ambivalent identification, see Goldberg, "The 400 Genders."

63. This process of learning has changed over time in relation to the normalization of gayness. As Dustin Bradley Goltz explains, many older gay men had "aunties" or "mothas" to introduce them to gay culture when it was more clandestine, whereas many younger gay and queer men now easily access—and reject—postmillennial gay culture without a guide. "'We're Not in Oz Anymore.'"

64. Stedman, *IRL*.

65. "Heteroflexible" is a start. See Ward, *Not Gay*.

66. Weeks, *The Problem with Work*, 202.

67. Weeks, 185.

68. Alex Espinoza details his disappointment in the West Hollywood gay club scene and his frustration that his Mexican friends were treated by white guys as "outlets for their own sexual kinks and fantasies." He writes, "[The club scene] required me to look and dress a certain way, and try as I might, I was never going to be as cute and desirable as my friends. In that space, nobody eyed me. Nobody wanted or needed me the way men in the restrooms, parks, and back alleys did." A few pages later he elaborates, "Cruising helped me realize that I was needed and wanted by men. My anatomy, I learned after a few hookups, was indeed unique. . . . Because in that world nobody cared whether I was

disabled. Nobody cared that I was poor or weak or socially awkward. They cared about only one thing." Espinoza is vague here: does he have a big dick? No gag reflex? Buns of steel? Is he capable of multiple, voluminous orgasms? Whatever the case, his experience seems to support Bersani's claim that in ideal cruising we shed our "social personality," while also raising questions about the relation of his bodily matter (and capacities) to his desirability. Is the "one thing" that Espinoza's admirers cared about unrelated to his social characteristics? Did his admirers truly not care about these characteristics, or did they just care more about something else? *Cruising*, 31, 33.

69. Dean, *Unlimited Intimacy*, 164. For more on categories and types in relation to gender, see Goldberg, "The 400 Genders."

70. Bersani, "Is the Rectum a Grave?," 206.

71. On sex as a solitary pursuit, see Phillips, *Monogamy*, 101.

72. The suspicion that otherness lurks within what appears to be sameness might be even more exciting (if unsettling), more tantalizing, more of an incitement to play for some people. Think of all the novels, films, and television shows in which a friend, lover, or family member is discovered to have an enormous secret, which then completely disturbs their relationships.

73. Phillips, *Unforbidden Pleasures*, 59.

74. Bersani and Phillips, *Intimacies*, 59. It was one of Freud's great accomplishments, Phillips writes, to abandon the religious discourse of good and evil and replace it with the secular discourse of acceptable and unacceptable desires: "For Freud, any moral clarity we have is a temporary suppression of the complexity of our desires." This shift makes it possible to attend to the way that ethical commitments can repress desires. *Unforbidden Pleasures*, 35.

75. As Richardson writes, "Much of the time spent cruising is not having sex but playing a cat-and-mouse game of nonverbal communication with potential sex partners/gay bashers/law enforcement." "Queering Edgework." This game can itself be enjoyable. As Shaka McGlotten observes, "Browsing is something you do to enjoy being in the flow of desire rather than trying to satiate it." *Virtual Intimacies*, 135.

Chapter 3

1. There are many gay hookup and dating apps and sites: Grindr, Scruff, Jackd, Sniffies, and so on. There are interesting and important differences between them, but that's not my concern here. When not describing the specific features of Grindr, I use "Grindr" as shorthand for them all.

2. To be more specific, the eroticized body is everything, as Mowlabocus argues. *Gaydar Culture*, 79. See also Goldberg, "Meet Markets."

3. As McGlotten writes, "Creating a profile forces one to attend to one's own desirability and to one's own desire. . . . *Virtual Intimacies*, 68. For more on the engineering of profiles, see "On Not Hooking Up" in *Virtual Intimacies* and " 'From the Web Comes the Man': Profiles, Identity and Embodiment in Gay Dating/Sex Websites" in Mowlabocus, *Gaydar Culture*.

4. " 'Party and Play,' " 266.

5. Caws, "To Hell and Back," 170.

6. Phillips, *Monogamy*, 7.

7. *That Man: Peter Berlin*.

8. "Towards a Pragmatics of Sexual Media/Networking Devices," 1328.

9. Phillips, *Monogamy*, 101.

10. This differentiates my approach from scholars like Mowlabocus who lean heavily on the concept of objectification in describing how gay men understand and respond to eroticized imagery online. For a history of the term "fetish" and its various uses, see "Fetishes" in Hillis, *Online a Lot of the Time*.

11. Although my parents identified as communists, and some of their friends were also communists, I use the softer "socialist" here, in part, because of Camp Kinderland, where "socialist" was the more popular ideological self-identification. With apologies to my parents, their friends, and my comrades at Kinderland, it makes no difference here.

12. For more on the uneasy relationship between socialists, communists, and "sexual dissidents" (including homosexuals) in the US pre-Stonewall, see Lecklider, *Love's Next Meeting*.

13. Hardy and Easton, *The Ethical Slut, Third Edition*.

14. For the record, Craig never seemed to care much about this. He was too psychoanalytically attuned, and maybe too much of a pervert, to sit in judgment.

15. See, for example Eng, *Racial Castration*; McBride, "It's a White Man's World."

16. Chu, "Did Sissy Porn Make Me Trans?," 6.

17. McClintock, *Imperial Leather*.

18. Bersani, "Is the Rectum a Grave?," 216.

19. McClintock, *Imperial Leather*, 184.

20. Dean, *Unlimited Intimacy*, 160.

21. See Dean, 148.

22. *Screen Love*, 122.

23. Cutler, *Labor's Time*.

24. Espinoza, *Cruising*, 38.

25. Phillips, *Missing Out*, 43.

26. Phillips, 183.

27. Althusser, "Ideology and Ideological State Apparatuses (Notes towards an Investigation)," 103.

Chapter 4

1. "Uses of Perversity," 273.
2. Dean and Lane, "Homosexuality & Psychoanalysis," 28.
3. *How To Be Gay*, 206.
4. Mowlabocus makes this point via Quentin Crisp's notion of the "great dark man." *Gaydar Culture*, 137.
5. In the context of online cruising, Robert Payne describes this as the "user's desire to fulfill the ideals invested in his profile, to merge with that persona, especially those elements of the persona most likely to receive recognition and affirmation within the culture of other users." "'Str8acting,'" 531.
6. My browsing process thus departs from Mowlabocus's characterization of users as looking at profiles "to discover the real person [on] the other side of the screen." *Gaydar Culture*, 114.
7. Payne, "'Str8acting.'"
8. Halperin, *How To Be Gay*, 49–50.
9. Gladwell, "Complexity and the Ten-Thousand-Hour Rule."
10. Louis, *The End of Eddy*, 143.
11. *How To Be Gay*, 210.
12. Salam, "What Is Toxic Masculinity?"
13. Salter, "The Problem with a Fight Against Toxic Masculinity." Simultaneously, a similar concept—"hegemonic masculinity"—was theorized by sociologist R. W. Connell and then widely adopted across the humanities and social sciences. It's reasonable to assume that "toxic masculinity" became the popular term because "toxic" is a common word and "hegemonic" is not. See Connell and Messerschmidt, "Hegemonic Masculinity."
14. Hall, "Controversial Proud Boys Embrace 'Western Values,' Reject Feminism and Political Correctness."
15. Ingraham.
16. For a description and critique of positive masculinity from a left perspective, see Whippman, "We Can Do Better Than Positive Masculinity."
17. Dean, "Sameness without Identity," 32.
18. I feel seen (and called out) by Mowlabocus's critique of the eroticization of class in relation to masculinity: "The fantasy of working-class heterosexual masculinity that pervades the cybercottage is politically problematic to say the least." *Gaydar Culture*, 144.
19. Chu, *Females*, 11; Halberstam, "Nice Trannies." Not to be defensive, but trans-friendly cruising bars do exist, as Billy Huff writes about in "On (Be)coming in Boystown."
20. Chu, *Females*, 13.
21. LaFleur, "Heterosexuality without Women."
22. Bersani, "Is the Rectum a Grave?," 212. For more on the female dick, see Hart, *Between the Body and the Flesh*.

23. Belcourt, Dust, and Gabriel, "Top or Bottom."

24. Manders, "The Renegades."

25. Halberstam, *Female Masculinity*, 1. To be certain, Halberstam doesn't exactly let female masculinity off the hook either, as when he critiques Gertrude Stein and Alice B. Toklas as reactionary, and notes that "Radclyffe Hall and other masculine women" participated "in early British fascist movements." *The Queer Art of Failure*, 151, 160.

26. Phillips, *Unforbidden Pleasures*, 24.

27. Bersani, "Is the Rectum a Grave?," 208. For more on the advent of the clone, see Halperin, *How To Be Gay*, 50–53.

28. Bersani, "Is the Rectum a Grave?," 209.

29. Halperin echoes this argument when he writes, "Gay male culture's virtue is to register—and then to resist—forms of social stratification that continue to structure our world. . . ." *How To Be Gay*, 208.

30. Marx, *Groucho and Me*, 321.

31. Bersani, "Is the Rectum a Grave?," 217.

32. *Homo Psyche*, 207.

33. Bersani, "Is the Rectum a Grave?," 218, 222.

34. Bersani, 206. Halberstam pursues this line of thinking in "'The Killer in Me Is the Killer in You': Homosexuality and Fascism" in *The Queer Art of Failure*.

35. Bersani, "Sociality and Sexuality," 648.

36. *Homo Psyche*, 3.

37. *The Twilight of Equality?*

38. As Tom Roach notes, Bersani's later work shifts toward theorizing "an ethical subject that develops according to the rhythms of an impersonal, expansive, and even cosmic narcissism." Roach, *Screen Love*, 20.

39. Chu and Berg, "Wanting Bad Things."

40. *Infinite Resignation*.

41. King, *It*, 787–88.

42. Nelson, *The Argonauts*, 93.

43. I'm reminded of Jamie Hakim's argument that male bodybuilding and selfie sharing is part of what he calls neoliberalism's "feminising axiomatic." See "The Spornosexual: The Affective Contradictions of Digital Male Body-Work in an Age of Austerity" in *Work That Body*. For an examination of musculature and masculinity, see Dyer, "Desire and Difference."

44. Sedgwick, "Gosh, Boy George, You Must Be Awfully Secure in Your Masculinity!" For an example of a taxonomic breakdown of various kinds masculinity, see Hakim, *Work That Body*, 135.

45. Sullivan, *Information for the Female to Male Crossdresser and Transsexual*.

46. Halperin, *How To Be Gay*, 317.

47. On the other hand, as Nguyen Tan Hoang observes, "The mainstream American gay male community . . . remains enamored with its butch tops and

butcher bottoms." *A View from the Bottom*, 10. Perhaps my desire is not so uncommon after all.

48. *Homos*, 112.

49. *Unlimited Intimacy*, 51. Jane Ward coins the term "anal resilience" to describe how being penetrated—as a man—might counterintuitively enhance one's masculinity. *Not Gay*, 43.

50. Dean, "Sameness without Identity," 34; Dean, *Unlimited Intimacy*, 163. See also Dollimore, "Desire and Difference."

51. Bersani, "Is the Rectum a Grave?," 209.

52. Bersani, "Sociability and Cruising," 16.

53. Benderson, *The Romanian*, 59.

54. Bersani, "Genital Chastity," 365.

Chapter 5

1. Bullock, "Peter Berlin."
2. "Consent in the Dark," 46.
3. Delany, *Times Square Red, Times Square Blue*, 187.
4. See Rudder, *Dataclysm*. That said, sexual desire can also defy norms of attractiveness, in part because sexuality has the mysterious and surprising power to transform the disgusting into the erotic—and vice versa—or at least to bring them into proximity.
5. Srinivasan, "Does Anyone Have the Right to Sex?"
6. Later in the book, McGlotten similarly characterizes Grindr as a "hypercompetitive erotic marketplace in which whiteness enjoys preeminence." *Virtual Intimacies*, 5, 61.
7. Or maybe we shouldn't place so much emphasis on desirability in the first place. In an interview, Mia Mingus values ugliness over beauty as a "pathway to intimacy." She observes, "People think beauty is something that will make you feel better; that everybody wants/needs to feel like they're beautiful. Because people can't sit with the reality of what their life is like. It's a band-aid, a life raft where they don't have to join you in the water themselves." ALOK and Mingus, "Why Ugliness Is Vital in the Age of Social Media."
8. Chu and Berg, "Wanting Bad Things."
9. Phillips, *Monogamy*, 113.
10. Irby, *Wow, No Thank You*, 75.
11. "Queer Critique, Queer Refusal," 127.
12. Binyam, "Letter of Recommendation."
13. "Community Guidelines."
14. See Phillips, *Unforbidden Pleasures*.
15. Phillips, 30.

16. See also Daroya, "'Not Into Chopsticks or Curries': Erotic Capital and the Psychic Life of Racism on Grindr."

Chapter 6

1. As cited by Bersani, "Is the Rectum a Grave?," 219.
2. Phillips, *Monogamy*, 70.
3. Bruhm, *Reflecting Narcissus*. See also Goldberg, "Through the Looking Glass."
4. Brooks, "The Devotion Leap."
5. See Goldberg, "Meet Markets."
6. As Kane Race argues, the key features of apps like Grindr—for example, location-based searching—"frame the sexual encounters they enable as 'no strings' or commitment-free." At the same time, "one-off encounters [may] spill over into other types of relations." For this reason, Race argues, we ought to understand the relations established through apps like Grindr in terms of "degrees of reciprocity, care, indebtedness, commitment, disregard, neglect and attachment" rather than a stark opposition between anonymity and bondedness. "Speculative Pragmatism and Intimate Arrangements," 501. The relationship I describe in the next chapter could be taken as evidence of this. For now, though, I'm less interested in these lived nuances than I am in the kind of ideal cruising about which Bersani writes and with which critics take issue.
7. *How To Be Gay*, 294.
8. For example (once again): Hardy and Easton, *The Ethical Slut, Third Edition*.
9. *Indifference to Difference*, 16.
10. Chu, "On Liking Women."
11. Roach, "Becoming Fungible"; McGlotten, *Virtual Intimacies*.
12. Grindr removed the ability to filter for "ethnicity" (i.e., race) in June 2020 in solidarity with the Black Lives Matter movement, or so the company claimed. "Grindr Removes 'ethnicity Filter' after Complaints."
13. Chu and Berg, "Wanting Bad Things."
14. "Like."
15. McGlotten makes a similar point in relation to the way that his interviewees—queer Black men—are either excluded by non-Black men on Grindr or else solicited insofar as they are willing and able to inhabit particular stereotypes. *Virtual Intimacies*, 69.
16. See Dean, "The Biopolitics of Pleasure"; Race, "The Use of Pleasure in Harm Reduction," 419.
17. Foucault, *The History of Sexuality, Vol. 1*, 157.
18. Bersani, *Homos*, 104.

19. Weeks, *The Problem with Work*, 176.

20. Muñoz, *Cruising Utopia*, 1.

21. As Muñoz writes in the introduction, "I do see an unlimited potentiality in actual queer sex, but books of criticism that simply glamorize the ontology of gay male cruising are more often than not simply boring," 18. Silvia Federici is more explicit in arguing that sex serves a palliative function under capitalism. See Tortorici, "More Smiles?"

22. Of course, there are many reasons—besides pleasure, or in addition to it—that people have sex: because they want to reproduce; they want to make the person they're having sex with feel good (perhaps for ethical or political reasons, as Jane Ward writes); they want to feel normal; they feel like they have to have sex in order to maintain a relationship; it gives them leverage in a relationship; it boosts their self-esteem; they're bored; they feel a compulsion to do it; it will give them social capital; they want to make someone else jealous, and so on. Ward, "The Straight Rules Don't Apply: Lesbian Sexual Ethics."

23. In his discussion of John Giorno's vivid, autobiographical descriptions of public sex, Muñoz similarly pivots quickly to the "powerful political impulse" he reads in the text, despite Giorno's own refusal to imbue cruising with ideology. *Cruising Utopia*, 36.

24. There is also a difference between feeling a sense of togetherness at a chemsex party and being a part of a community, despite Jamie Hakim's use of the term "collective" to describe the former. There are, in other words, significant differences between all the various ways we can be in relation to other people. It is for this reason, I suspect, that Hakim says little about the sex in chemsex and focuses instead on what he calls "collective intimacies." Hakim, *Work That Body*, 126. This is not to downplay the extent to which group sex gatherings might involve activities such as "chatting and chilling, filming sex, watching porn, collective browsing, various forms of consumption and the exchange of information about other individuals and encounters," as Kane Race notes. Nor is it to deny that these activities can "change the texture of stranger sociability." It is simply to inquire about the scholarly desire for sex to yield collectivity. "Speculative Pragmatism and Intimate Arrangements," 506–7.

25. Muñoz, *Cruising Utopia*, 64; *Antisocial Media*, 30.

26. Phillips, *Unforbidden Pleasures*, 1.

27. *Virtual Intimacies*, 73. For Snediker, queer optimism is "situated . . . firmly in the present." *Queer Optimism*, 16.

28. *Screen Love*, xv.

29. Wilson, "Open Season."

30. *Homo Psyche*, 16. In this sense, using Grindr might be as much about the pleasures of manipulating its interface in the present as it is about the sex that may result, as Roach argues. *Screen Love*, 62.

Chapter 7

1. "Hookups" is a relatively new option, replacing the more time-specific and euphemistic category "right now."

2. A campy how-to guide, *The Beginner's Guide to Cruising* (1964), might beg to differ. From a section titled "The Attack": "If you suggest to him abruptly to come to bed with you, all you will get is a fist in the belly and the end of your acquaintance. You must lead him towards it gradually and almost imperceptibly. You must induce him to make one tiny concession after the other. Each of such concessions, in itself, will mean nothing. Added together they will represent his total capitulation." *The Beginner's Guide to Cruising*, 33. Or from another section, titled "Tools and Equipment": "[The cruiser] will have to submit the gay to hot and cold sentimental showers, to alternate rather frequently periods of great affection with others of relative indifference. Inevitably he will made to suffer and this is why a certain amount of cruelty on the part of the cruiser is necessary" (6). To be fair, the cruising described in this guide is more akin to the game playing I describe in this chapter than it is to the spontaneous, anonymous sex that characterizes cruising in the contemporary sense of the term. I imagine that this evolution of cruising is a function of the normalization of gayness.

3. Fein and Schneider, *Not Your Mother's Rules*, 42–43.

4. Brian A. Horton's definition of play is useful here: "[A] particular kind of joking, unserious, or ephemeral disposition that can temporarily suspend and confuse hierarchy, relations of power, and perhaps even the law itself." "The Police and the Policed: Queer Crossings in a Mumbai Bathroom," 54.

5. The extent to which game playing is seen as acceptable or not also surely depends on the social positions of the players (and of those judging) and the context in which they find themselves.

6. "The Game." Ten years after its publication, Strauss critiqued the tactics of manipulation described in *The Game* as "unhealthy," while standing by it as an accurate representation of a former version of himself. Gilsinan, "The Game at 10: Reflections from a Recovering Pickup Artist."

7. Tziallas, "Gamified Eroticism."

8. For more on Simmel, play, and sociability, see Bersani, "Sociability and Cruising"; Race, " 'Party and Play.' "

9. See Kipnis, *Against Love*.

10. Berlant, "Against Sexual Scandal."

11. This argument could easily be used to critique the desire for intimacy.

12. Phillips, *Missing Out*, 63.

13. As Dean writes (following Foucault), "[T]here are no pleasures that are *not* contaminated by power. . . ." See "The Biopolitics of Pleasure," 481. For this reason, Alex Espinoza's defensive claim that cruising is "devoid of the power

dynamics that plague heterosexual interactions and exists outside of traditional hierarchies" and that "it is founded on equality" is dubious. *Cruising*, 32, 200.

14. Juul, *The Art of Failure*.
15. Freud, "Beyond the Pleasure Principle, Group Psychology and Other Works (1920–1922)," 14–15.
16. Reid, "Crushed. . . ."
17. Fish, *There's No Such Thing as Free Speech*, 278.
18. Bersani, "Is the Rectum a Grave?," 217.
19. Bersani, *Homos*, 95.
20. Phillips, *Missing Out*, 79.
21. Perel, "Safety vs. Adventure in Relationships."
22. *Homo Psyche*, 16.
23. "Constitutive antagonisms" is a concept coined by Jonathan Cutler in the context of labor movements. *Labor's Time*, 13.

Bibliography

Acocella, Joan. "This Is Your Life." *New Yorker*, February 18, 2013. https://www.newyorker.com/magazine/2013/02/25/this-is-your-life-2.
Adeyemi, Kemi, Kareem Khubchandani, and Ramon H. Rivera-Servera. "Introduction." In *Queer Nightlife*, edited by Kemi Adeyemi, Kareem Khubchandani, and Ramon H. Rivera-Servera, 1–16. Ann Arbor: University of Michigan Press, 2021.
———, eds. *Queer Nightlife*. Ann Arbor: University of Michigan Press, 2021.
Adorno, Theodor W. "On the Fetish Character in Music and the Regression of Listening." In *Essays on Music*, edited by Richard Leppert, translated by Susan H. Gillespie, 288–317. Berkeley: University of California Press, 2002.
Adorno, Theodor W., and George Simpson. "On Popular Music." In *Essays on Music*, edited by Richard Leppert, translated by Susan H. Gillespie, 437–69. Berkeley: University of California Press, 2002.
Ahmed, Sara. "Orientations: Toward a Queer Phenomenology." *GLQ: A Journal of Lesbian and Gay Studies* 12, no. 4 (2006): 543–74.
ALOK, and Mia Mingus. "Why Ugliness Is Vital in the Age of Social Media." *them*, October 26, 2018. https://www.them.us/story/ugliness-disability-mia-mingus.
Althusser, Louis. "Ideology and Ideological State Apparatuses (Notes Towards an Investigation)." In *The Anthropology of the State: A Reader*, edited by Aradhana Sharma and Anil Gupta, 9:86–111. Malden, MA: Blackwell Publishing, 2006.
Amin, Kadji. "We Are All Nonbinary: A Brief History of Accidents." *Representations* 158, no. 1 (2022): 106–19.
Ashtor, Gila. *Homo Psyche: On Queer Theory and Erotophobia*. New York: Fordham University Press, 2021.
Attwood, Feona, Jamie Hakim, and Alison Winch. "Mediated Intimacies: Bodies, Technologies and Relationships." *Journal of Gender Studies* 26, no. 3 (May 4, 2017): 249–53.
BBC News. "Grindr Removes 'Ethnicity Filter' After Complaints." June 1, 2020, sec. Technology. https://www.bbc.com/news/technology-52886167.

Bibliography

Belcourt, Billy-Ray, George Dust, and Kay Gabriel. "Top or Bottom: How Do We Desire?" *The New Inquiry*, October 10, 2018. https://thenewinquiry.com/top-or-bottom-how-do-we-desire/.

Benderson, Bruce. *The Romanian: Story of an Obsession*. New York: Penguin, 2006.

Berger, Peter L. *Invitation to Sociology: A Humanistic Perspective*. New York: Doubleday, 1963.

Berlant, Lauren. "Against Sexual Scandal." *The Nation*, March 12, 2008. https://www.thenation.com/article/archive/against-sexual-scandal/.

———. "Intimacy: A Special Issue." *Critical Inquiry* 24, no. 2 (January 1998): 281–88.

Bersani, Leo. "Genital Chastity." In *Homosexuality and Psychoanalysis*, edited by Tim Dean and Christopher Lane, 351–66. Chicago: University of Chicago Press, 2001.

———. *Homos*. Cambridge: Harvard University Press, 1996.

———. "Is the Rectum a Grave?" *October* 43 (1987): 197–222.

———. "Sociability and Cruising." *UMBR(a) Sameness*, no. 1 (2002): 9–23.

———. "Sociality and Sexuality." *Critical Inquiry* 26, no. 4 (2000): 641–56.

Bersani, Leo, and Adam Phillips. *Intimacies*. Chicago: University of Chicago Press, 2008.

"Beyond Red vs. Blue: The Political Typology." Washington, DC: Pew Research Center, November 9, 2021. https://www.pewresearch.org/politics/2021/11/09/beyond-red-vs-blue-the-political-typology-2/.

Binyam, Maya. "Letter of Recommendation: Ghosting." *New York Times*, August 3, 2017. https://www.nytimes.com/2017/08/03/magazine/letter-of-recommendation-ghosting.html.

Brooks, David. "The Devotion Leap." *New York Times*, January 22, 2015. https://www.nytimes.com/2015/01/23/opinion/david-brooks-the-devotion-leap.html.

Bruhm, Steven. *Reflecting Narcissus: A Queer Aesthetic*. Minneapolis: University of Minnesota Press, 2001.

Bullock, Michael. "Peter Berlin." *Apartamento Magazine*, 2019. https://www.apartamentomagazine.com/stories/peter-berlin/.

Califia, Pat. *Public Sex: The Culture of Radical Sex*. San Francisco: Cleis Press, 2000.

Caserio, Robert L., Lee Edelman, Judith Halberstam, José Esteban Muñoz, and Tim Dean. "The Antisocial Thesis in Queer Theory." *PMLA* 121, no. 3 (5/06): 819–28.

Caws, Peter. "To Hell and Back: Sartre on (and in) Analysis with Freud." *Sartre Studies International* 11, no. 1/2 (2005): 166–76.

Cheves, Alexander. "Consent in the Dark." In *Unsafe Words: Queering Consent in the #MeToo Era*, edited by Trevor Hoppe and Shantel Gabrieal Buggs, 41–52. New Brunswick, NJ: Rutgers University Press, 2023.

Chu, Andrea Long. "Did Sissy Porn Make Me Trans?" Queer Disruptions 2 (conference), March 1–2, 2018. New York: Columbia University.

———. *Females*. New York: Verso Books, 2019.

---. "On Liking Women." *N+1*, Winter 2018. https://nplusonemag.com/issue-30/essays/on-liking-women/.

Chu, Andrea Long, and Anastasia Berg. "Wanting Bad Things: Andrea Long Chu Responds to Amia Srinivasan." *The Point Magazine*, July 18, 2018. https://thepointmag.com/dialogue/wanting-bad-things-andrea-long-chu-responds-amia-srinivasan/.

Clough, Patricia Ticineto. *The End(s) of Ethnography: From Realism to Social Criticism*. New York: Peter Lang, 1998.

Cohen, Cathy J. "Punks, Bulldaggers, and Welfare Queens: The Radical Potential of Queer Politics?" *GLQ: A Journal of Lesbian and Gay Studies* 3, no. 4 (May 1, 1997): 437–65.

Connell, R. W., and James W. Messerschmidt. "Hegemonic Masculinity: Rethinking the Concept." *Gender & Society* 19, no. 6 (December 2005): 829–59.

Corey, Frederick C., and Thomas K. Nakayama. "Sextext." *Text and Performance Quarterly*, January 1, 1997.

Cutler, Jonathan. *Labor's Time: Shorter Hours, the UAW, and the Struggle for American Unionism*. Philadelphia: Temple University Press, 2008.

Daniel, Drew. "All Sound Is Queer." *The Wire* 33, no. 3 (2011): 43–46.

Daroya, Emerich. "'Not Into Chopsticks or Curries': Erotic Capital and the Psychic Life of Racism on Grindr." In *The Psychic Life of Racism in Gay Men's Communities*, edited by Damien W. Riggs, 67–80. New York: Lexington Books, 2018.

Davis, Oliver, and Tim Dean. *Hatred of Sex*. Lincoln: University of Nebraska Press, 2022.

De Lauretis, Teresa. "Queer Texts, Bad Habits, and the Issue of a Future." *GLQ: A Journal of Lesbian and Gay Studies* 17, no. 2–3 (2011): 243–63.

Dean, Tim. "Homosexuality and the Problem of Otherness." In *Homosexuality and Psychoanalysis*, edited by Tim Dean and Christopher Lane, 120–43. Chicago: University of Chicago Press, 2001.

---. "Sameness without Identity." *UMBR(a)* Sameness, no. 1 (2002): 25–41.

---. "Sex and the Aesthetics of Existence." *PMLA* 125, no. 2 (2010): 387–92.

---. "The Biopolitics of Pleasure." *South Atlantic Quarterly* 111, no. 3 (2012): 477–96.

---. *Unlimited Intimacy: Reflections on the Subculture of Barebacking*. Chicago: University of Chicago Press, 2009.

---. "Uses of Perversity: Commentary on Saketopoulou's 'To Suffer Pleasure.'" *Studies in Gender and Sexuality* 15, no. 4 (2014): 269–77.

Dean, Tim, Hal Foster, Kaja Silverman, and Leo Bersani. "A Conversation with Leo Bersani." *October* 82 (1997): 3–16.

Dean, Tim, and Christopher Lane. "Homosexuality and Psychoanalysis: An Introduction." In *Homosexuality & Psychoanalysis*, edited by Tim Dean and Christopher Lane, 3–42. Chicago: University Of Chicago Press, 2001.

Delany, Samuel R. *Times Square Red, Times Square Blue*. New York: New York University Press, 1999.

Deleuze, Gilles, and Felix Guatarri. *A Thousand Plateaus: Capitalism and Schizophrenia*. Minneapolis: University of Minnesota Press, 2007.

Dollimore, Jonathan. "Desire and Difference: Homosexuality, Race, Masculinity." In *Race and the Subject of Masculinities*, edited by Harilaos Stecopoulos and Michael Uebel, 17–44. Durham: Duke University Press, 1997.

Duggan, Lisa. *The Twilight of Equality?: Neoliberalism, Cultural Politics, and the Attack on Democracy*. Boston: Beacon Press, 2012.

Dyer, Richard. "The White Man's Muscles." In *Race and the Subject of Masculinities*, edited by Harilaos Stecopoulos and Michael Uebel, 286–314. Durham: Duke University Press, 1997.

Edelman, Lee. *Bad Education: Why Queer Theory Teaches Us Nothing*. Durham: Duke University Press, 2022.

———. "Men's Room." In *Stud: Architectures of Masculinity*, edited by Joel Sanders, 152–61. Princeton, NJ: Princeton Architectural Press, 1996.

———. *No Future: Queer Theory and the Death Drive*. Durham: Duke University Press, 2004.

Eng, David L. *Racial Castration: Managing Masculinity in Asian America*. Durham: Duke University Press, 2001.

Espinoza, Alex. *Cruising: An Intimate History of a Radical Pastime*. Los Angeles: Unnamed Press, 2019.

Fanon, Frantz. *Black Skin, White Masks*. Translated by Charles Lamm Markmann. New York: Grove Press, 1967.

Fein, Ellen, and Sherrie Schneider. *Not Your Mother's Rules: The New Secrets for Dating*. New York: Grand Central Publishing, 2013.

Ferguson, Roderick A. *One-Dimensional Queer*. Medford, MA: Polity Press, 2019.

Fine, Gary Alan, and Ugo Corte. "Group Pleasures: Collaborative Commitments, Shared Narrative, and the Sociology of Fun." *Sociological Theory* 35, no. 1 (March 1, 2017): 64–86.

Fischel, Joseph J. *Screw Consent: A Better Politics of Sexual Justice*. Oakland: University of California Press, 2019.

Fish, Stanley. *There's No Such Thing As Free Speech: And It's a Good Thing, Too*. New York: Oxford University Press, 1994.

Flatley, Jonathan. "Like: Collecting and Collectivity." *October*, no. 132 (Spring 2010): 71–98.

Foucault, Michel. *Foucault Live: Collected Interviews, 1961–1984*. Edited by Sylvère Lotringer, translated by Lysa Hochroth and John Johnston. New York: Semiotext(e), 1996.

———. *The History of Sexuality, Vol. 1: An Introduction*. Reissue ed. New York: Vintage Books, 1978.

Franzen, Jonathan. "Liking Is for Cowards. Go for What Hurts." *New York Times*, May 28, 2011. http://www.nytimes.com/2011/05/29/opinion/29franzen.html.

Freud, Sigmund. "Beyond the Pleasure Principle, Group Psychology and Other Works (1920–1922)." In *The Standard Edition of the Complete Psychological Works of Sigmund Freud*. Vol. XVIII, edited by James Strachey. London: The Hogarth Press, 1964.

———. "On the Universal Tendency to Debasement in the Sphere of Love." In *The Standard Edition of the Complete Psychological Works of Sigmund Freud*. Vol. XI, edited by James Strachey. London: The Hogarth Press, 1964.

Gilsinan, Kathy. "The Game at 10: Reflections from a Recovering Pickup Artist." *The Atlantic*, October 13, 2015. https://www.theatlantic.com/entertainment/archive/2015/10/neil-strauss-the-game/409789/.

Gladwell, Malcolm. "Complexity and the Ten-Thousand-Hour Rule." *New Yorker*. Accessed February 3, 2021. https://www.newyorker.com/sports/sporting-scene/complexity-and-the-ten-thousand-hour-rule.

Goldberg, Greg. *Antisocial Media: Anxious Labor in the Digital Economy*. New York: New York University Press, 2018.

———. "Lust Room." *GLQ: A Journal of Lesbian and Gay Studies* 31, no. 1 (Winter 2025).

———. "Meet Markets: Grindr and the Politics of Objectifying Others." *Convergence* 26, no. 2 (July 19, 2018): 253–68.

———. "The 400 Genders." *Cultural Critique*, no. 126 (Winter 2025).

———. "Through the Looking Glass: The Queer Narcissism of Selfies." *Social Media + Society* 3, no. 1 (March 27, 2017).

Goltz, Dustin Bradley. "'We're Not in Oz Anymore': Shifting Generational Perspectives and Tensions of Gay Community, Identity, and Future." *Journal of Homosexuality* 61, no. 11 (November 2, 2014): 1503–28.

Grindr. "Community Guidelines." Accessed February 3, 2021. https://www.grindr.com/community-guidelines/?lang=en-US.

Habib, Conner. "Rest Stop Confidential." *Salon*, March 29, 2012. https://www.salon.com/2012/03/29/rest_stop_confidential/.

Hakim, Jamie. *Work That Body: Male Bodies in Digital Culture*. New York: Rowman & Littlefield, 2019.

Hakim, Jamie, and Kane Race. "The Gay Scientist: Kane Race on the Unexpected Possibilities of Experimental Intimacies." *Sexualities* 26, no. 5–6 (September 1, 2023): 574–84.

Halberstam, Jack. *Female Masculinity*. Durham: Duke University Press, 1998.

———. "Nice Trannies." *Transgender Studies Quarterly* 7, no. 3 (2020): 321–31.

Halberstam, Judith. *The Queer Art of Failure*. Durham: Duke University Press, 2011.

Hall, Alexandra. "Controversial Proud Boys Embrace 'Western Values,' Reject Feminism and Political Correctness." *Wisconsin Watch*, November 26, 2017. https://www.wisconsinwatch.org/2017/11/proud-boys-group-wisconsin/.

Halperin, David M. *How To Be Gay*. Cambridge: Harvard University Press, 2012.

———. "Introduction." In *The War on Sex*, edited by David M. Halperin and Trevor Hoppe, 1–61. Durham: Duke University Press, 2017.

Hardy, Janet W., and Dossie Easton. *The Ethical Slut, Third Edition: A Practical Guide to Polyamory, Open Relationships, and Other Freedoms in Sex and Love*. Berkeley, CA: Clarkson Potter/Ten Speed, 2017.

Hart, Lynda. *Between the Body and the Flesh: Performing Sadomasochism*. New York: Columbia University Press, 1998.

Hillis, Ken. *Online a Lot of the Time: Ritual, Fetish, Sign*. Durham: Duke University Press, 2009.

Holmes, Dave, Patrick O'Byrne, and Stuart J. Murray. "Faceless Sex: Glory Holes and Sexual Assemblages." *Nursing Philosophy* 11, no. 4 (September 1, 2010): 250–59.

Hoppe, Trevor. "Lost in the Dark—Or How I Learned to Queer Consent." In *Unsafe Words: Queering Consent in the #MeToo Era*, edited by Trevor Hoppe and Shantel Gabrieal Buggs, 53–64. New Brunswick, NJ: Rutgers University Press, 2023.

Horton, Brian A. "The Police and the Policed: Queer Crossings in a Mumbai Bathroom." In *Queer Nightlife*, edited by Kemi Adeyemi, Kareem Khubchandani, and Ramon H. Rivera-Servera, 53–64. Ann Arbor: University of Michigan Press, 2021.

Huff, Billy. "On [Be]Coming in Boystown." *Journal of Autoethnography* 3, no. 4 (October 1, 2022): 427–44.

Humphreys, Laud. "Tearoom Trade: Impersonal Sex in Public Places." In *Public Sex/Gay Space*, edited by William L. Leap. New York: Columbia University Press, 1999.

Hunt, A. J., P. Weatherburn, F. C. I. Hickson, P. M. Davies, T. J. McManus, and A. P. M. Coxon. "Changes in Condom Use by Gay Men." *AIDS Care* 5, no. 4 (October 1, 1993): 439–48.

Ingraham: The War Against Men, 2019. https://www.youtube.com/watch?v=BHlNfpni6oM&feature=emb_logo&ab_channel=FoxNews.

Irby, Samantha. *Wow, No Thank You.: Essays*. New York: Knopf Doubleday, 2020.

Johnson, E. Patrick. "'Quare' Studies, or (Almost) Everything I Know About Queer Studies I Learned from My Grandmother." *Text and Performance Quarterly* 21, no. 1 (2001): 1–25.

Juul, Jesper. *The Art of Failure: An Essay on the Pain of Playing Video Games*. Cambridge: MIT Press, 2013.

Kerri, Amanda. "The Lowest Form of Humor: Bottoming Jokes from Straight Comedians." *Advocate*, April 18, 2018. https://www.advocate.com/commentary/2018/4/18/lowest-form-humor-bottoming-jokes-straight-comedians.

King, Stephen. *It*. New York: Viking, 1986.

Kipnis, Laura. *Against Love: A Polemic*. New York: Knopf Doubleday, 2004.

LaFleur, Greta. "Heterosexuality Without Women." *Los Angeles Review of Books*, May 20, 2019. https://blog.lareviewofbooks.org/essays/heterosexuality-without-women/.

Lecklider, Aaron. *Love's Next Meeting: The Forgotten History of Homosexuality and the Left in American Culture*. Oakland: University of California Press, 2021.

Lorde, Audre. *A Burst of Light: And Other Essays*. Mineola, NY: Ixia Press, 2017.

Louis, Édouard. *The End of Eddy*. New York: Farrar, Straus and Giroux, 2017.

Love, Heather. "Queer Critique, Queer Refusal." In *The Great Refusal: Herbert Marcuse and Contemporary Social Movements*, edited by Andrew Lamas, Todd Wolfson, and Peter N. Funke, 118–31. Philadelphia: Temple University Press, 2017.

———. *Underdogs: Social Deviance and Queer Theory*. Chicago: University of Chicago Press, 2021.

Manalansan, Martin F., IV. "The 'Stuff' of Archives: Mess, Migration, and Queer Lives." *Radical History Review* 2014, no. 120 (October 1, 2014): 94–107.

Manders, Kerry. "The Renegades." *New York Times*, April 13, 2020. https://www.nytimes.com/interactive/2020/04/13/t-magazine/butch-stud-lesbian.html.

Marriott, David. "On Racial Fetishism." *Qui Parle: Critical Humanities and Social Sciences* 18, no. 2 (2010): 215–48.

Marshall, George. *The Beginner's Guide to Cruising*. Washington, DC: Guild Book Service, 1964.

Marx, Groucho. *Groucho and Me*. New York: B. Geis Associates, 1959.

Marx, Karl. "Theses on Feuerbach." In *Karl Marx and Frederick Engels Selected Works: Volume One*, translated by W. Lough, 13–15. Moscow: Progress Publishers, 1969.

McBride, Dwight. "It's a White Man's World." In *Why I Hate Abercrombie & Fitch: Essays on Race and Sexuality*, 41:88–131. New York: New York University Press, 2005.

McClintock, Anne. *Imperial Leather: Race, Gender, and Sexuality in the Colonial Contest*. New York: Routledge, 1995.

McGlotten, Shaka. *Virtual Intimacies: Media, Affect, and Queer Sociality*. Albany: State University of New York Press, 2013.

Menon, Madhavi. *Indifference to Difference: On Queer Universalism*. Minneapolis: University of Minnesota Press, 2015.

Morris, Wesley. "My Mustache, My Self." *New York Times*, October 14, 2020. https://www.nytimes.com/2020/10/14/magazine/quarantine-mustache.html.

Mowlabocus, Sharif. *Gaydar Culture: Gay Men, Technology and Embodiment in the Digital Age*. New York: Routledge, 2016.

Muñoz, José Esteban. *Cruising Utopia: The Then and There of Queer Futurity*. New York: New York University Press, 2009.

Murray, Stephen O. "Self Size and Observable Sex." In *Public Sex/Gay Space*, edited by William L. Leap, 157–86. New York: Columbia University Press, 1999.

Musser, Amber Jamilla. *Sensational Flesh: Race, Power, and Masochism*. New York: New York University Press, 2014.

Musto, Michael. "Gay Dance Clubs on the Wane in the Age of Grindr." *New York Times*, April 26, 2016. http://www.nytimes.com/2016/04/28/fashion/gay-dance-clubs-grindr.html.

Nelson, Maggie. *On Freedom: Four Songs of Care and Constraint*. Minneapolis: Graywolf Press, 2021.

———. *The Argonauts*. Minneapolis: Graywolf Press, 2015.

Nguyen, Tan Hoang. *A View from the Bottom: Asian American Masculinity and Sexual Representation*. Durham: Duke University Press, 2014.

Page, River. "Don't Be a Bigot, It's 'Houseless' Now." *Pirate Wires* (blog), May 14, 2023. https://www.piratewires.com/p/houseless.

Parker-Pope, Tara. "Why Self-Care Isn't Selfish." *New York Times*, January 6, 2021, sec. Well. https://www.nytimes.com/2021/01/06/well/live/why-self-care-isnt-selfish.html.

Payne, Robert. "'Str8acting.'" *Social Semiotics* 17, no. 4 (December 1, 2007): 525–38.

———. *The Promiscuity of Network Culture: Queer Theory and Digital Media*. New York: Routledge, 2014.

Perel, Esther. "Safety vs. Adventure in Relationships." *Medium*, November 10, 2014. https://medium.com/@EstherPerel/safety-vs-adventure-in-relationships-188b1292bb3a.

———. "The Secret to Desire in a Long-Term Relationship." TED, February 2013. https://www.ted.com/talks/esther_perel_the_secret_to_desire_in_a_long_term_relationship.

Peters, Torrey. *Detransition, Baby*. New York: Random House, 2021.

Phillips, Adam. *Missing Out: In Praise of the Unlived Life*. New York: Farrar, Straus and Giroux, 2013.

———. *Monogamy*. New York: Vintage, 2010.

———. *Unforbidden Pleasures*. New York: Farrar, Straus and Giroux, 2015.

Poushter, Jacob, and Nicholas Kent. "The Global Divide on Homosexuality Persists." Pew Research Center, June 25, 2020. https://www.pewresearch.org/global/2020/06/25/global-divide-on-homosexuality-persists/.

Race, Kane. "'Party and Play': Online Hook-up Devices and the Emergence of PNP Practices among Gay Men." *Sexualities* 18, no. 3 (March 1, 2015): 253–75.

———. "Speculative Pragmatism and Intimate Arrangements: Online Hook-up Devices in Gay Life." *Culture, Health & Sexuality* 17, no. 4 (2015): 496–511.

———. "The Use of Pleasure in Harm Reduction: Perspectives from the History of Sexuality." *International Journal of Drug Policy* 19, no. 5 (October 1, 2008): 417–23.

———. "Thinking with Pleasure: Experimenting with Drugs and Drug Research." *International Journal of Drug Policy* 49 (November 1, 2017): 144–49.

———. "Towards a Pragmatics of Sexual Media/Networking Devices." *Sexualities* 21, no. 8 (December 1, 2018): 1325–30.

Reid, Tiana. "Crushed. . . ." *The New Inquiry* (blog), March 7, 2018. https://thenewinquiry.com/crushed/.

Richardson, Diane. "Constructing Lesbian Sexualities." In *Feminism and Sexuality*, edited by Stevi Jackson and Sue Scott, 276–86. Edinburgh: Edinburgh University Press, 1996.

Richardson, Jacob W. "Queering Edgework: An Autoethnographic Account of Cruising for Sex." *Journal of Autoethnography* 5, no. 1 (2024): 95–114.

River Page [@river_is_nice]. Tweet. *Twitter*, May 9, 2022. https://twitter.com/river_is_nice/status/1523724406819680256.

Roach, Tom. "Becoming Fungible: Queer Intimacies in Social Media." *Qui Parle: Critical Humanities and Social Sciences* 23, no. 2 (April 29, 2015): 55–87.

———. *Screen Love: Queer Intimacies in the Grindr Era*. Albany: State University of New York Press, 2021.

Rogers, Thomas. "The Pines' Summer of Discontent." *New York Magazine*, July 20, 2012. https://nymag.com/news/intelligencer/grindr-fire-island-2012-7/.

Rubin, Gayle. "Thinking Sex: Notes for a Radical Theory of the Politics of Sexuality." In *Social Perspectives in Lesbian and Gay Studies: A Reader*, edited by Peter M. Nardi and Beth E. Schneider, 100–33. New York: Routledge, 1984.

Rudder, Christian. *Dataclysm: Love, Sex, Race, and Identity—What Our Online Lives Tell Us About Our Offline Selves*. New York: Broadway Books, 2014.

Saketopoulou, Avgi. "To Suffer Pleasure: The Shattering of the Ego as the Psychic Labor of Perverse Sexuality." *Studies in Gender and Sexuality* 15, no. 4 (2014): 254–68.

Salam, Maya. "What Is Toxic Masculinity?" *New York Times*, January 22, 2019, sec. U.S. https://www.nytimes.com/2019/01/22/us/toxic-masculinity.html.

Salter, Michael. "The Problem with a Fight Against Toxic Masculinity." *The Atlantic*, February 27, 2019. https://www.theatlantic.com/health/archive/2019/02/toxic-masculinity-history/583411/.

Sedgwick, Eve Kosofsky. "Gosh, Boy George, You Must Be Awfully Secure in Your Masculinity!" In *Constructing Masculinities*, edited by Maurice Berger, Brian Wallis, and Simon Watson, 11–20. New York: Routledge, 1995.

Seidman, Steven. *The Social Construction of Sexuality*. New York: W. W. Norton, 2010.

Smith, Zack. "John Waters on the Mainstreaming of Gay Culture." *INDY Week*, September 19, 2007. http://indyweek.com/culture/screen/john-waters-mainstreaming-gay-culture/.

Snediker, Michael D. *Queer Optimism: Lyric Personhood and Other Felicitous Persuasions*. Minneapolis: University of Minnesota Press, 2009.

Srinivasan, Amia. "Does Anyone Have the Right to Sex?" *London Review of Books*, March 22, 2018. https://www.lrb.co.uk/the-paper/v40/n06/amia-srinivasan/does-anyone-have-the-right-to-sex.

Bibliography

Stedman, Chris. *IRL: Finding Realness, Meaning, and Belonging in Our Digital Lives*. Minneapolis: Broadleaf Books, 2020.

Strauss, Neil. *The Game: Penetrating the Secret Society of Pickup Artists*. New York: ReganBooks, 2005.

Sullivan, Louis. *Information for the Female to Male Crossdresser and Transsexual*. 2nd ed. San Francisco, 1985.

Thacker, Eugene. *Infinite Resignation*. London: Repeater, 2018.

Tortorici, Dayna. "More Smiles? More Money." *N+1*, Fall 2013. https://www.nplusonemag.com/issue-17/reviews/more-smiles-more-money/.

Tuhkanen, Mikko. "Rigorously Speculating: An Interview with Leo Bersani." In *Leo Bersani: Queer Theory and Beyond*, edited by Mikko Tuhkanen. Albany: State University of New York Press, 2014.

Tushinski, Jim, dir. *That Man: Peter Berlin*, 2005. 81 min.

Tziallas, Evangelos. "Gamified Eroticism: Gay Male 'Social Networking' Applications and Self-Pornography." *Sexuality & Culture* 19, no. 4 (December 1, 2015): 759–75.

Ward, Jane. *Not Gay: Sex between Straight White Men*. New York: New York University Press, 2015.

———. "The Straight Rules Don't Apply: Lesbian Sexual Ethics." In *Unsafe Words: Queering Consent in the #MeToo Era*, edited by Trevor Hoppe and Shantel Gabrieal Buggs, 65–72. New Brunswick, NJ: Rutgers University Press, 2023.

Warner, Michael. "Queer and Then?" *Chronicle of Higher Education*, January 1, 2012. https://www.chronicle.com/article/queer-and-then/.

Weeks, Kathi. *The Problem with Work: Feminism, Marxism, Antiwork Politics, and Postwork Imaginaries*. Durham: Duke University Press, 2011.

Weiss, Margot, ed. "Queer Theories from Somewhere: Situated Knowledges and Other Queer Empiricisms." In *Unsettling Queer Anthropology: Foundations, Reorientations, and Departures*, 53–76. Durham: Duke University Press, 2024.

Whippman, Ruth. "We Can Do Better Than 'Positive Masculinity.'" *New York Times*, October 8, 2024, sec. Opinion. https://www.nytimes.com/2024/10/08/opinion/positive-masculinity.html.

Wiegman, Robyn. *Object Lessons*. Next Wave: New Directions in Women's Studies. Durham: Duke University Press, 2012.

Wilson, Jennifer. "Open Season." *New Yorker*, 2024. https://www.newyorker.com/magazine/2024/01/01/american-poly-christopher-gleason-book-review-more-a-memoir-of-open-marriage-molly-roden-winter.

Zurn, Perry. *Curiosity and Power: The Politics of Inquiry*. Minneapolis: University of Minnesota Press, 2021.

Index

abundance, 90, 91–92, 93
Acocella, Joan, 29
Adorno, Theodor, 11
aggrandizement, joint, 54
Ahmed, Sara, 18
AIDS Care (journal), 5
AIDS crisis (1980s), 5, 8–9, 65
"All Sound Is Queer" (Daniel), 32
alternative relationship styles, 104
Althusser, Louis, 56, 60
ambivalence, 111
American culture, 25, 27
American Psychological Association, 61
anonymity, of cruising, 59
anonymous sex, 26. *See also* cruising
anti-identitarianism, 10
Antisocial Media (Goldberg), 96
antisocial sex, xiv
antisocial thesis, 34
The Argonauts (Nelson), 71
The Art of Failure (Juul), 110
Ashtor, Gila, 66, 99, 114, 121n40
Asian men, 86
Atkinson, Ti-Grace, 10
attraction, 38–39, 43, 44
attractiveness, 92, 130n4
authoritarianism, 10

bad behavior, 83

baldness, 44
Barthes, Roland, 122
bathhouses, 30, 39, 64
BDSM, 112
"bear," 39
beauty, 130n6
Becker, Howard, 11
The Beginner's Guide to Cruising (Marshall), 133n2
behavior, moralization of, 83–84
Belcourt, Billy-Ray, 63, 73
Benderson, Bruce, 75
Berg, Anastasia, 80
Berger, Peter, 18
Berghain (Berlin club), 26–27
Berlant, Lauren, 66, 107
Berlin (Germany), 26–27
Berlin, Peter, 48, 78–79
Bersani, Leo, xvii, 10, 28, 38–41, 76, 118n21, 124n43, 124n51
  on bathhouses, 64
  on BDSM, 112
  "Genital Chastity," 75
  homophobia and, 9, 67
  on impersonal intimacy, 30–31
  on internalized homophobia, 66
  "Is the Rectum a Grave?," 8–9, 27, 39, 65
  on less information in cruising, 48
  on masculinity, 65

Bersani, Leo *(continued)*
  on penis envy, 52
  on psychoanalysis, 93–94
  self-shattering and, 67, 122n12
Beyond the Pleasure Principle (Freud), 111
Binyam, Maya, 83, 84
BIPOC, 32
bisexual men, 5, 101
Black Lives Matter, 131n12
Black men, 121n37
Blackness, 35
blue-collar men, 57
bodily matter, 38
body hair, 72
bodybuilding, 72
"born this way" rhetoric, 36
bottoming, 58
  masculinity and, 9, 56, 74, 76
  pleasure and, 76
  self-shattering and, 66
Brokeback Mountain (film), 103
Bronx, New York, 4
Brooks, David, 89
Brown, Wendy, 38
Butler, Judith, 55
Buttigieg, Chasten Glezman, 62
Buttigieg, Pete, xiii, 62

Califia-Rice, Patrick, 5
Camp Kinderland, 14–15, 127n11
capitalism, 11
"Castro clone," 90
casual sex, 89
Cena, John, 55
chemsex, 119n10, 132n24
Cheves, Alexander, 79
Christians, gay, 51
Chu, Andrea Long, xvii, 15, 51–52, 68, 80, 83, 90, 92
  Females, 62
  "On Liking Women," 82
clothing, 30

Club Q mass shooting, 67
Cohen, Cathy J., 33
collective intimacies, 132n24
collective politics, 97
coming out, xii, xiv
commitment, 88
condoms, 5
consent, 120n32
conservatives, 89
constitutive antagonisms, 134n23
contact
  forms of, 24
  interracial, 7
  interclass, 7
control
  giving up, 41
  social, 31, 88
conversion therapy, 59
Corey, Frederick C., xv
Cosby, Bill, 62
Craig (friend), 51
Critical Mass, 15, 51
cruising, xi–xii, xiv, 38, 41, 90, 104, 117n3. *See also specific topics*
  anonymity of, 59
  as cyclical process, 53–54
  impersonal intimacy of, 30
  in-person, 21, 48
  motivation for, 59
  at New York Botanical Garden, 4–5
  online, 128n5
  promiscuity and, 88
  in public restrooms, 2–4, 5–6
  rejection and, 77, 87
  at rest areas, 1–2
  risk in, 18
Cruising Utopia (Muñoz), 95–96
"cub," 39, 101
culture
  American, 25, 27
  of Grindr, 49
  non-hetero, 36
  queer, 104

Cutler, Jonathan, 54, 134n23

"daddy," 45, 46
Daniel, Drew, 32
dating, online, 89
Davis, Oliver, xv, 13, 35
De Lauretis, Teresa, xiii
Dean, Tim, xv, xvii, 13, 32, 39, 61, 120n25, 123n25
   on desire, 53
   on identity, 123n26
   on public sex, 23
"deep" masculinity, 61
Delany, Samuel, 7–8, 10–11, 26–27, 79, 91, 96
Deleuze, Gilles, 122n10
DeMent, Iris, xvi
depth, 49
DeSantis, Ron, xiii
desexualization, 62
desire, xiii–xiv, 34, 39, 94, 110
   abundance and, 92
   as "bad," xv, xvii
   for blue-collar men, 57
   defending, 8
   emergent, 22
   Foucault on, 93
   Freud and, 53
   meaning and, 86
   moralization of, 84
   objects of, 44, 50
   racialized gender and, 79
   social, 52
   as specific, 53
destigmatization, 7
detachment, 87, 89
The Devil Wears Prada (film), 82
difference, 28
differentiation, 31
dissatisfaction, 95
Dolezal, Rachel, 35
domination, 112
"Don't Say Gay" law, xiii, 67

Duggan, Lisa, 67
Dworkin, Andrea, 10

Edelman, Lee, 2–3, 10–11, 33, 124n52
emergent desire, 22
The End of Eddy (Louis), 60
Epstein, Jeffrey, 62
Espinoza, Alex, xiv, xvii, 54, 125n68
estrangement, 30
"ethical slut," xii
ethics
   ethically grounded politics, 16
   politics without, 13
   sex as ethical, 12
ethnicity, 131n12
external stimulation, as pleasure, 23

familiarity, 59
Fanon, Frantz, 28–29, 124n52
fantasy, 48, 93
Female Masculinity (Halberstam), 63
Females (Chu), 62
femininity, 59, 60, 73
feminism, on Internet, 15
Ferguson, Roderick E., xii
fetishism/fetishes, 28, 31, 51–53
Feuerbach, Ludwig, 16
Fire Island, 20
Fischel, Joe, 120n32
Fish, Stanley, 111
Flatley, Jonathan, xvi, 92
forms of contact, 24
Foucault, Michel, 9, 11, 32, 87, 93, 98, 123n32
Frank, Jon, 68
Franzen, Jonathan, 25–26
Freud, Sigmund, 2, 23, 52, 68–69, 74, 110, 114, 126n74
   Beyond the Pleasure Principle, 111
   desire and, 53
"fuckable," 80

The Game (Strauss), 107

"gay," 33–36
gay Christians, 51
"gay clone," 64, 90
gay liberation, xii
gender
   public restrooms and, 2
   "queer" and, 31
   racialized, 79
"Genital Chastity" (Bersani), 75
Germany, 26–27
ghosting, 78, 81
Gladwell, Malcolm, 60
glory hole, 30–31
Goffman, Irving, 55
Goldberg, Greg, 96
Goltz, Dustin Bradley, 125n63
Greenblatt, Stephen, 55
Grindr, xviii, 20–21, 39, 59, 81, 101–104, 126n1, 130n6
   abundance and, 90, 91–92
   community guidelines of, 84
   culture of, 49
   ethnicity on, 131n12
   "masc for masc," 63
   mutual interest on, 47
   objectification and, 49–50
   pictures on, 43–47
   rejection on, 78
   topping and, 73
Guatarri, Felix, 122n10

Habib, Conner, 5
Hakim, Jamie, 119n10, 129n43, 132n24
Halberstam, Jack, 16, 62, 63, 129n25
Halperin, David M., 59, 60, 89
hearing, 22–23
hedonism, 11, 12
hegemonic masculinity, 71, 128n13
heterogeneity, 36, 72
heterosexuality, 10
"Heterosexuality without Women" (LaFleur), 62

HIV, 5
Hocquenghem, Guy, 32
Holmes, Dave, 30–31, 124n40
homogeneity, 90
homonormativity, 67
homophobia, 10–11, 33–35, 37, 62, 69, 85
   Bersani and, 9, 67
   internalized, 65–66
"The Homosexual Community" (Hooker), xvi
Hooker, Evelyn, xvi
Horton, Brian A., 133n4
Huff, Billy, 121n37
Hughes, John, 57
Humphreys, Laud, 21

identification
   inaccurate replication and, 75
   "queer" and, 31
identity, 31, 51–52
   attachment to, 37
   -based oppression, 33
   Dean on, 123n26
   dismantling, 35
   granting of, xiv
   "queer" and, 32
   "queer" as umbrella, xiii
identity politics, 38
impersonal intimacy, 27–28, 30–31
inaccurate replication, 75
Indigenous Americans, 61
individual personalities, 30
Information for the Female-to-Male Crossdresser and Transsexual (Sullivan), 72
Ingraham, Laura, 61
in-person cruising, 21, 48
interclass contact, 7
internalized homophobia, 65–66
Internet, feminism on, 15
interpersonal relations, 28
interracial contact, 7

intersectionality, xv, 118n19
intersubjective violence, 31
intimacy, 25–26
  collective, 132n24
  impersonal, 27–28, 30–31
Irby, Samantha, 81
Irigaray, Luce, 52, 124n52
"Is the Rectum a Grave?" (Bersani), 8–9, 27, 39, 65
It (King), 69–70

Jeremy (fuck buddy), 74, 76, 101–103, 108–113
Jersey Shore (TV series), 57
Johnson, E. Patrick, 34
joint aggrandizement, 54
Juul, Jesper, 110

King, Stephen, 69–70
Kristeva, Julia, 124n52

labor, 14, 120n26
LaFleur, Greta, 62, 63
Lane, Christopher, 59
language, 39
Leggler, Casey, 63
Levinas, Emmanuel, 124n40
Louis, Edouard, 60
love, 25–26
Love, Heather, xvi, 81

MacKinnon, Catharine, 10
Malibou, Catherine, 124n52
Manders, Kerry, 63
Marshall, George, 133n2
Marx, Groucho, 65
Marx, Karl, 11, 16, 68, 96, 114
"masc for masc," 63
masculinity, 60, 68, 70
  amplification of, 59
  Bersani on, 65
  bisexual men and, 101
  body hair and, 72

  bottoming and, 9, 56, 74, 76
  eroticization of, 58–59, 62–64, 66
  hegemonic, 71, 128n13
  heterogeneity and, 72
  positive, 61, 64
  soft, 53
  submission and, 112
  topping and, 63, 73
  toxic, 61, 64
  violating, 56
  working-class, 52
masochism, 111
mass shootings, 67
McClintock, Anne, 52
McGlotten, Shaka, xvii, 18, 20, 26, 79, 98, 127n3, 130n6
McInnes, Gavin, 61
meaning
  bodily matter and, 38–39
  desire and, 86
men who have sex with men (MSM), 58, 60, 66, 117n5
Menon, Madhavi, 33, 89, 124n56
men's area, 19
men's movement, New Age, 61
men's room, 3
#MeToo, 120n32
Mingus, Mia, 26, 130n6
Minoxidil, 44
monogamy, 46, 51, 94, 98–99
Monogamy (Phillips), 88
moralism, 10, 17, 82
morality, 41
moralization
  of behavior, 83–84
  of desire, 84
  of sex, xiv
Morris, Wesley, 35
Mosholu Parkway, 4
Moten, Fred, 124n52
The Motion of Light in Water (Delany), 96
Mowlabocus, Sharif, 122n3, 127n10

MSM. *See* men who have sex with
    men
Muñoz, José Esteban, 33–34, 95–97
Murray, Stuart J., 30–31, 124n40
musculature, 72
Musser, Amber Jamilla, 118n19
Musto, Michael, 20

Nakayama, Thomas K., xv
narcissism, 31, 88
Nelson, Maggie, 13, 22, 71
neoliberalism, 129n43
neutrality, xvi
New Age men's movement, 61
The New Inquiry, 63
New York Botanical Garden, 4–5
New York Magazine, 20
New York Times, 20, 25, 61, 63, 83, 89
Nietzsche, Friedrich, 37
nightlife, queer, 119n14
No Exit (Sartre), 45–46
non-hetero cultures, 36
non-monogamy, 51
non-normative sex, policing of, 7
non-normativity, sexual, 36
nonviolence, 41
norms, 3
    photographic, 46
    social control and, 88
Not Your Mother's Rules, 105–106, 109
nuclear family, 89

objectification, 49–50, 90, 127n3
O'Byrne, Patrick, 30–31, 124n40
"On Liking Women" (Chu), 82
online cruising, 128n5. *See also*
    Grindr
online dating, 89
ontological negation, 34
open relationships, 98–99
opioids, 11
oppression, identity-based, 33

optimism, queer, 98
otherness, 28, 38, 41

pain, 23
parent-child relations, 55
participatory surveillance, 107
Pascal, Blaise, 56
"passing," 59
pathologization, 6, 8, 26, 114, 119n6
patriarchy, 9–10
Payne, Robert, 59, 128n5
penis envy, 52
Perel, Esther, 18, 114
personalities, 30
personhood, 51–52
Peters, Torrey, 16
Pew Research Center, 117n5
Phillips, Adam, xv, xvii, 46, 49, 64,
    98, 108, 113
    Acocella and, 29
    on detachment, 88
    on morality, 41
    on moralization, 84
    on parent-child relations, 55
photographic norms, 46
pictures, on Grindr, 43–47
"playing games," 107–108, 133n5
"playing hard to get," 104–108, 113
pleasure, xiii–xiv, 34, 42, 94, 110–111
    as "bad," xv, xvii
    bottoming and, 76
    defending, 8
    estrangement and, 30
    external stimulation as, 23
    Foucault on, 93
    good versus bad kinds of, 120n25
    in otherness, 41
    responsibility and, 12
    self-care and, 12
    as self-shattering, 122n13
    of sociology, 18
    of submission, 112

of transgression, xi, 84
uneasiness with, 11
"polar bear," 39
policing, of non-normative sex, 7
political demonstrations, 14
politics, 17, 42
   appeal to, 8
   collective, 97
   ethically grounded, 16
   without ethics, 13
polyamory, 98–99, 104
positive masculinity, 61, 64
power, 110
powerlessness, 112
pride, xiv
promiscuity, 88, 94
psychoanalysis, 29–30, 93–94, 108, 110, 123n32
public restrooms, 2–6
public sex, xi–xii, 20, 23
public sphere, 7
Pulse nightclub mass shooting, 67

"queer," xii–xiii, 31–32, 37
queer culture, 104
queer left, 63–64
queer nightlife, 119n14
queer optimism, 98
queer theory, xii, xv, 88
queer universalism, 33–34, 36–37, 124n56
queerness, 34

Race, Kane, xv, xvii, 11, 29, 45, 49, 120n31, 131n6
Rachel (friend), 68, 78
racialized gender, 79
reading, xvii–xviii
Reddy, Chandan, 118n19
Reid, Tiana, 111
rejection, 40, 77–78, 79, 87
Republican National Convention, 15, 51

responsibility, pleasure and, 12
ressentiment, 38
rest areas, 1–2, 18
restrooms, public, 2–6
Revolutionary Communist Party, 14
Rich, Adrienne, 10
risk, 18
Roach, Tom, xvii, 10, 32, 54, 89, 98, 129n38
role play, 45
romantic relationships, 102
Rubin, Gayle, xiii, 7–10, 17
Ruffalo, Mark, 53

St. Mark's Baths, 96
Saketopoulou, Avgi, 10
Salam, Maya, 61
Salter, Michael, 61
sameness, 28
Sartre, Jean-Paul, 45–46
Saturday Night Live (TV program), xiii
scarcity, 93
secondary sex characteristic, body hair as, 72
Sedgwick, Eve, xii, xvii, 71–72, 74, 121n40
Seidman, Steven, 31–32
self-advocacy, 13, 82
self-care, 12
self-evaluation, 35
self-fashioning, 55
self-help, 65
self-image, 45
selfishness, 84
self-pornification, 107
self-shattering, 65–67, 122n12, 122n13
Sexton, Jared, 124n52
sexual assault law, 120n32
sexual freedom, xii
sexual non-normativity, 36
sexual speculation, 45
sexual variation, 7

shame, 8, 17
sight, 22–23
Simmel, Georg, 107
Simpson, O. J., 35
S/M, 64
Snediker, Michael, 98
social characteristics, 79–80
social control, 31, 88
social desires, 52
social justice, 51
social life, segregation of, 7
social personalities, 30
social relations, 28
socialism, 50
sociology, 18, 29
soft masculinity, 53
solitary pervert model, 96–97
Spitzer, Eliot, 107
Srinivasan, Amia, 10, 79–80, 86
status quo, 95
Stedman, Chris, 36
stigma, xiv, 7, 85
Stonewall, 6
"straight-acting," 59, 65, 75
strangers, 48, 123n25
Strauss, Neill, 107
subjectivity, 32
submission, pleasure of, 112
Sullivan, Lou, 72
surface, 49

Tea, Michelle, 13
Tearoom Trade (Humphreys), 21
Thacker, Eugene, 68
"Thinking Sex" (Rubin), xiii, 7
Time (magazine), 62
topping, 63, 73, 76
touch, 22–23
toxic masculinity, 61, 64
transgression, 17
  pleasure of, xi, 84
  romanticizing, 3

Tziallas, Evangelos, 107

ugliness, 26, 81, 130n6
"unfuckable," 80, 85, 86
universalism, queer, 33–34, 36–37, 124n56
urinals, 3–4
utopianism, 94–95, 98

victim narratives, 85
violence
  intersubjective, 31
  mass shootings, 67
  nonviolence, 41
  of white supremacy, 83

"war on men," 61
Ward, Jane, 132n22
Warhol, Andy, xvi, 90, 92
Warner, Michael, xii, 32, 104
"warrior" masculinity, 61
Weeks, Kathi, 37, 95
Weinstein, Harvey, 62
Weiss, Margot, 29
Wesleyan University, 32
West Hollywood gay club scene, 125n68
White, Betty, 74
white supremacy, 83
whiteness, xiv
Wilde, Oscar, 98, 114
Willis, Ellen, 10, 12
women, 52, 62, 74, 101, 105, 109
Woods, Tiger, 35
working-class masculinity, 52
writing, xvii–xviii
Wynter, Sylvia, 124n52

You Can Count on Me (film), 53
YouTube, 72

Zurn, Perry, 17